The Tragedy Series

the TRAGEDY

SERIES

Secret Lobster Claws and Other Misfortunes

BENJAMIN DEWEY

THOMAS DUNNE BOOKS
ST. MARTIN'S GRIFFIN ⚓ NEW YORK

THOMAS DUNNE BOOKS.
An imprint of St. Martin's Press.

www.thomasdunnebooks.com
www.stmartins.com

Designed by Jonathan Bennett

Library of Congress Cataloging-in-Publication Data is available upon request.

ISBN 978-1-250-06062-4 (paper over board)
ISBN 978-1-4668-6608-9 (e-book)

St. Martin's Griffin books may be purchased for educational, business, or promotional use. For information on bulk purchases, please contact the Macmillan Corporate and Premium Sales Department at 1-800-221-7945, extension 5442, or write to specialmarkets@macmillan.com.

First Edition: March 2015

10 9 8 7 6 5 4 3 2 1

Dedications

For my Father, Robert Alan Dewey, who taught me that even in the midst of profound loss and genuine tragedy one can find joy, solace, and lessons in humor.

It is from him that I derived my love of history, fine art, working with one's hands, surreal humor, and well-groomed facial hair. His lifelong appreciation of ancient cultures, objects, and locales made an indelible impression on me. He was my harshest critic and, in the end, my biggest supporter.

I miss you every day, Dad.

For my Mother, Lynne Christine Fischer, who inculcated me with profound empathy for all things, even inanimate objects. It is a quality that allows me to see the heart in hammers, narrate the inner lives of all animals, and experience a reluctance to throw out cereal boxes with lovable characters depicted on them.

She laughs the hardest at my jokes, always appreciates my work, and never doubted my wish to draw for a living. I love you, Mom. Thanks for everything.

And, for my dearest Wife, Lindsey Anne L. Ellis.

It is because of you that I wake in the morning with all joy that one human heart can hold. I am a better man because of your presence in my life and what I make is improved as a result of your influence, honesty, and assistance.

Many of the cartoons contained herein are directly inspired by our interactions, verbal exchanges, and the patient review, rejection, and/or acceptance of my weirdest notions.

You are my constant sadness reprieve. I love you.

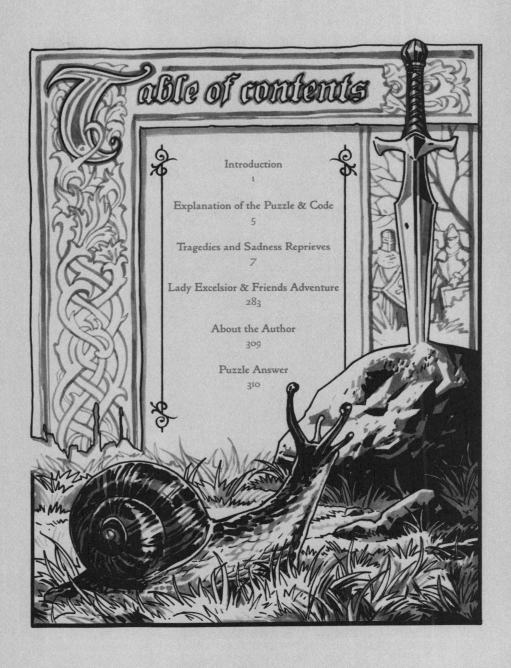

Table of contents

HELLO, READERS, and welcome to this comprehensive collection of melancholy tableaus that I provide for your instruction and enjoyment. "How did this sequence come to be?" you might ask. That is a fine and well-phrased question. Like many artistic endeavors, I undertook this project after agreeing to play chess with a known ursine psychopath and winning despite warnings of his competitive nature. The subsequent brush with death, convalescence, recovery, and eventual but reluctant friendship that resulted from my ill-advised victory dance taught me a valuable lesson. As the great philosopher Poplockrates once said, mid headspin, "Per Aspera Ad Astra." He was referring to the effects of his dizziness but the truth that emerged from his mumblings remains a salient point. It is through aeronautical failure, mistakes with fire, and other awkward tumbles upon the tightrope of life that we learn to reach our full stature.

Take these vignettes of comic-sadness to heart. Commit them to memory and avoid the fate of those less-fortunate bunglers, hubristic sea captains, and other disaster-prone eukaryotes with whom you share this grand, ongoing pageant of mystery. With the extra time not spent weeping over your crushing disappointments, I suggest you take up a productive activity or develop a skill that properly applied brings joy to others like a hybrid of bakery and earnest portraiture or pie'traiture. Every moment that you heed the counterexamples found within these pages is one spent avoiding the judgment of unfriendly bees while simultaneously experiencing what the Germans call "Schadenfruede," which, I have come to understand, is something like watching your nemesis trip over their favorite Fabergé egg into a pile of pies, all of which you hate. Learning to avoid mistakes in this way, in other words, has its pleasures.

The Bard of Avon once wrote that "When we are born, we cry that we are come to this great stage of fools" and he was correct. By means of psychic transference via a mentally gifted beetle associate, I have learned that the youngest amongst us are profoundly disappointed by most of our actions. Let us remedy this sad state of affairs and begin crafting a new phase of existence that elevates us all to the status of that brave giraffe who was the first to summit Earth's tallest peak and then ascend bodily to the realm where Zeus gifts terrestrial heroes with elegant medals and pastries crafted in their likenesses.

Excelsior,
Most sincerely,
BD

EXPLANATION OF THE PUZZLE & CODE

Dearest Readers,

I am an avid game and puzzle enthusiast. As such, I wanted to share my passion with those of you readers who are so inclined. In the last 100 cartoons (starting with tragedy 401 and ending with tragedy 500) I placed little clues for the eagle-eyed and fox-like to find among the captions and intertwined with the illustrations. The code consists of dots and dots with dashes. The unaccompanied dots represent garden-variety clues while the dots with dashes represent important breaks in the puzzle.

It is a passage from a favoite novel of mine. The reader who correctly answered this riddle, citing the exact quote, author and work from which it originates was to receive an artistic confection crafted by your humble servant and inspired by that winning sleuth's most significant waltzes in the Realm of King Morpheus. At the time of this writing, it has remained unsolved and possibly forgotten by the weary sailors on the ever-churning sea of passing days.

You, Sir or Madam, may investigate this mystery for yourself and do your best to unravel the Gordian Knot that I have laid tangled herein to delight and vex you. In the later pages of this work you will find the proper sequence of letters and the solution. I hope that you will not rush to that index point and simply unwrap this intellectual present in the fashion of a decadent human child, instead, rather like a noble, hibernating animal, you will accrue a vast collection of mind-morsels that when combined, make for a decadent feast for your frontal lobe as it enters a solution, joy will permeate your heart like the coming of a long delayed spring.

I wish you the best of luck and, may the result of your labors, the hidden rumination, be a shibboleth among those of us who care for all the delicious enigmas that this world may offer in the course of our lives including that greatest conundrum of all:

"What are we here for?"

Yours, cordially,
BD

Tragedies and
Sadness Reprieves

TRAGEDY # 1

SHE THINKS THIS IS AS BAD AS IT GETS

TRAGEDY #2

PUSHED DOWN STAIRS
BY GREAT APE

TRAGEDY # 3

THE BEES ALL HATE
YOUR NEW SPECTACLES

TRAGEDY # 4

BUNNY READ A BUNCH OF SAD BOOKS;
NOW SHE CAN'T STOP CRYING

BENJAMIN DEWEY

TRAGEDY#5

INDOOR ORCHIDS PLAGUED BY SURVIVORS' GUILT

TRAGEDY#6

SASQUATCH REGULARLY DOUBTS HIS OWN EXISTENCE

TRAGEDY #7

PERAMBULATOR FIRE

TRAGEDY #8

LEVEL OF TRUST IN THE COMMUNITY AT ALL-TIME LOW AFTER A RECENT 'BODYSNATCHER' INCIDENT

BENJAMIN DEWEY

TRAGEDY # 9

AXEPOCALYPSE

TRAGEDY # 10

SOMETIMES ONE MUST SHARE A POD WITH SOME REAL DUDS

TRAGEDY # 11

SUBMERSIBLE
COMMANDEERED
BY BEARS

TRAGEDY # 12

ONE MYSTERY THAT THE GREAT
DETECTIVE COULD NEVER SOLVE:
WHAT'S WRONG WITH KIDS THESE DAYS?

TRAGEDY #13

THEN HE DISCOVERED WHY NO OTHERS HAD COMPLETED THE QUEST

TRAGEDY #14

SECRET LOBSTER CLAWS

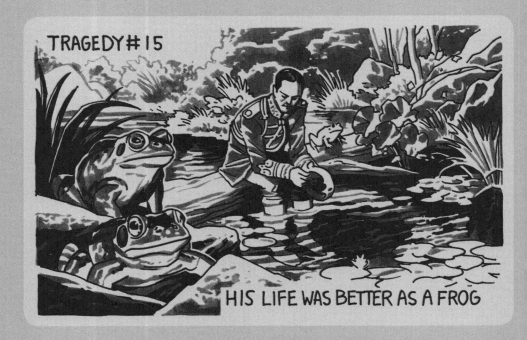

BENJAMIN DEWEY

TRAGEDY #17

PERPETUALLY DEADLOCKED
OVER DINNER OPTIONS

TRAGEDY #18

SENSITIVE CLOUD'S PRIDE WOUNDED
BY UNFLATTERING COMPARISONS

SADNESS REPRIEVE FIG. A

THERE IS MORE THAN ONE PERFECT FIT FOR EVERYONE

TRAGEDY # 19

RECURRENT SANDWICH WRENCH

BENJAMIN DEWEY

TRAGEDY #20

HER CALM CONTEMPLATION CORNER IS COMPROMISED BY CACOPHONOUS CADS

TRAGEDY #21

SOURCE OF OMNIPRESENT MAPLE ODOR AS YET UNIDENTIFIED

TRAGEDY # 22

EFFECTIVE YET UNORTHODOX FITNESS REGIMEN DESTINED FOR OBSCURITY

TRAGEDY # 23

KOALA FAUX PAS

BENJAMIN DEWEY

TRAGEDY #24

HIS PEACEFUL REIGN WAS CUT SHORT BY HIGH TIDE

TRAGEDY #25

HER MUSE WON'T MOVE ON FROM DEATH AND DOUGHNUTS

TRAGEDY #26

SHE BELIEVES THAT HE'S INNOCENT BUT DRAWS THE LINE AT HARBORING A FUGITIVE

TRAGEDY #27

UNBEATABLE YETI BARRED FROM ALL SUBSEQUENT COMPETITION

BENJAMIN DEWEY

TRAGEDY # 28

EXTREME SHUSHING-SQUAD BEGINS
CRACKING DOWN ON AUDIBLE PAGE TURNING

TRAGEDY # 29

FARMER THINKS HE PLANTED TURNIP SEEDS

TRAGEDY # 30

LOG MISSES BEING PART OF A TREE

TRAGEDY # 31

HUMPBACK DISENCHANTED WITH HIS 'CLASSIC' MATERIAL

TRAGEDY #32

EVEN THE RAREST AND MOST EXQUISITE OF GEARS STILL SERVES THE MACHINE

TRAGEDY #33

ONION SHARES ALL YOUR SECRETS

TRAGEDY #34

YOUNG MANTIS NEVER KNEW HIS DAD AND HIS MOM WON'T TALK ABOUT IT

TRAGEDY #35

HER COSTUME WAS A CONVERSATION TOPIC;
HER HEROISM WENT TOTALLY UNMENTIONED

BENJAMIN DEWEY

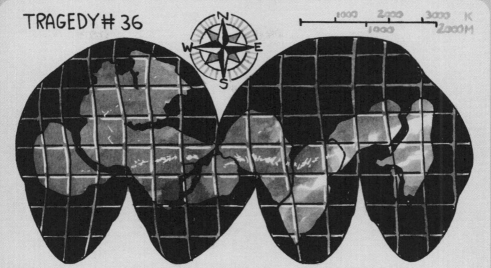

TRAGEDY # 36

THE RIFTS BETWEEN THEM LED TO A SLOW AND MESSY SEPARATION

TRAGEDY # 37

HYPOCHONDRIAC ROMANCE PEAKS AT CHASTE STARING

TRAGEDY #38

THE BLOBFISH ALWAYS SHOW UP
WHEN YOU'RE TRYING TO EAT YOGURT

SADNESS REPRIEVE FIG. B.

SMALL FRIEND, TALL FRIEND

BENJAMIN DEWEY

TRAGEDY # 39

IMPRESSIONABLE GARGOYLE HAS NOBODY TO LOOK UP TO

TRAGEDY #40

UNREQUITED LOAF

BENJAMIN DEWEY

TRAGEDY #42

WALK IN THE PARK IS UNEXPECTEDLY ARDUOUS

TRAGEDY #43

WOBBLY CAULDRON

BENJAMIN DEWEY

TRAGEDY # 44

ERUDITE RAM STANDS ALONE IN HIS EMBRACE OF THE DIALECTIC

TRAGEDY # 45

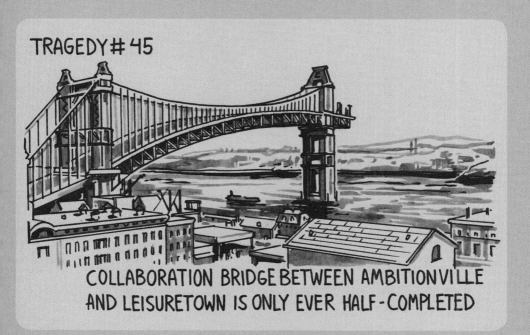

COLLABORATION BRIDGE BETWEEN AMBITIONVILLE
AND LEISURETOWN IS ONLY EVER HALF-COMPLETED

TRAGEDY # 46

POOR BABY, FORTUNATE DADDY

TRAGEDY # 47

THE STARS THAT SHE WISHED UPON WENT SUPERNOVA WEEKS AGO

BENJAMIN DEWEY

TRAGEDY #48

THE SKELETONS IN HER CLOSET HAVE BEEN MAKING
ILL-FITTING ALTERATIONS TO HER WARDROBE

TRAGEDY #49

'SPITTOON LAGOON' SPAWNS A VENGEFUL TERROR

TRAGEDY #50

THE ARMOR DOESN'T SHIELD HIM FROM CHARACTER ATTACKS

TRAGEDY #51

AFTER YEARS OF DRIFTING APART, THIS STARING
CONTEST IS ALL THE BUZZARD BROTHERS HAVE LEFT

BENJAMIN DEWEY

TRAGEDY #52

HEAD STUCK
IN DIVE HELMET
DURING WEDDING

TRAGEDY #53

ARGUMENT OVER SASH & SLOGAN SELECTION
DISINTEGRATES EMU/SUFFRAGETTE ALLIANCE

TRAGEDY # 54

HER DAILY LIFE & RECURRING NIGHTMARE BECOME INDISTINGUISHABLE

TRAGEDY # 55

SPIRIT QUEST RESULTS DEFY DEFINITIVE ANALYSIS

BENJAMIN DEWEY

TRAGEDY # 56

SHE HAD IMAGINED SOMETHING MORE GRAND
WHEN THEY PROPOSED A 'RACE AROUND THE GLOBE'

TRAGEDY # 57

THE ONLY ONE WORTHY OF THE
SWORD HAS NO HANDS TO GRASP IT

TRAGEDY # 58

NEIGHBORING ISLAND'S DECLARATION OF WAR
MISINTERPRETED AS INVITATION TO BEACH PARTY

SADNESS REPRIEVE FIG. C.

HE LOVES EVERY ASPECT OF HER

BENJAMIN DEWEY

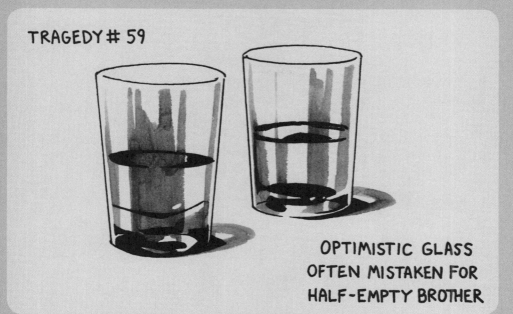

TRAGEDY # 59

OPTIMISTIC GLASS
OFTEN MISTAKEN FOR
HALF-EMPTY BROTHER

TRAGEDY # 60

THE GAZELLES RESPOND NEGATIVELY TO BATH TIME

TRAGEDY # 61

WRONG CASTLE

TRAGEDY # 62

THEREAFTER, THE RIVER CONTINUED RISING;
THE TOWN REGRETTED BANISHING THE BEAVERS

BENJAMIN DEWEY

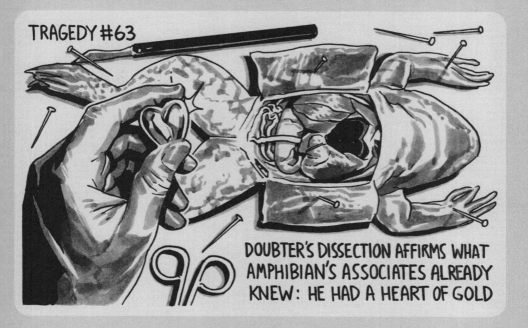

TRAGEDY #63

DOUBTER'S DISSECTION AFFIRMS WHAT AMPHIBIAN'S ASSOCIATES ALREADY KNEW: HE HAD A HEART OF GOLD

TRAGEDY # 64

ICE QUEEN CAN NEVER IMBIBE HOT COFFEE

TRAGEDY # 65

THE INHERITANCE COMES WITH A RESPONSIBILITY

TRAGEDY # 66

PERILOUS TURN
IN CYCLING TRYST

TRAGEDY #67

RECLUSIVE PARAKEET'S DISMISSAL OF EXCITING
INVITATIONS IRKS HIS ENVIOUS ATTENDANTS

TRAGEDY #68

INAPPROPRIATE BUBBLES COMPROMISE PEACE PROCESS

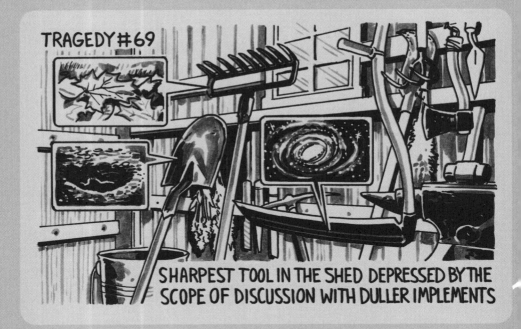

TRAGEDY #69

SHARPEST TOOL IN THE SHED DEPRESSED BY THE SCOPE OF DISCUSSION WITH DULLER IMPLEMENTS

TRAGEDY# 70

VIKING CHIEF ROUSED FROM NIGHTMARE

BENJAMIN DEWEY

TRAGEDY # 71

NARY A ONE OF THEM REMEMBERED JAM FOR THE CRUMPETS

TRAGEDY # 72

TINY MISANTHROPE BURDENED WITH AN ADORABLE FORM

TRAGEDY #73

THOSE WHO WANDER INTO THE SECRET MANATEE-MEETING COVE NEVER EMERGE AGAIN

TRAGEDY #74

NEW BOOKCASE DOESN'T SHARE YOUR TASTE

TRAGEDY #75

SIRENS' FAN BASE HAS DWINDLED

TRAGEDY #76

MIND-GREMLINS REPLACE A CHERISHED CHILDHOOD
RECOLLECTION WITH AN OBNOXIOUS EARWORM

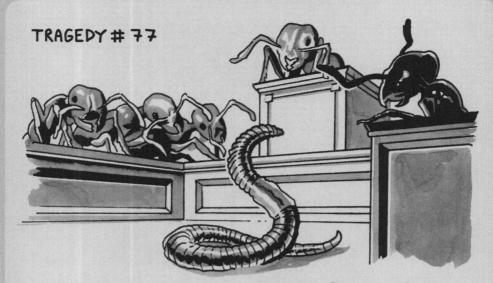

TRAGEDY # 77

TRIAL BY FIRE ANTS

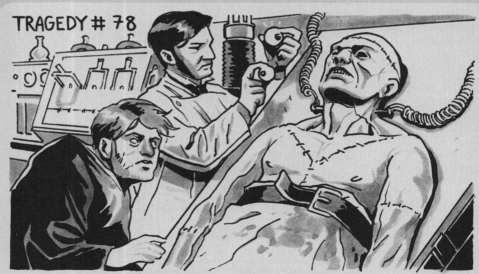

TRAGEDY # 78

ADDING GOOGLY-EYES ONLY MADE THE CREATURE CREEPIER

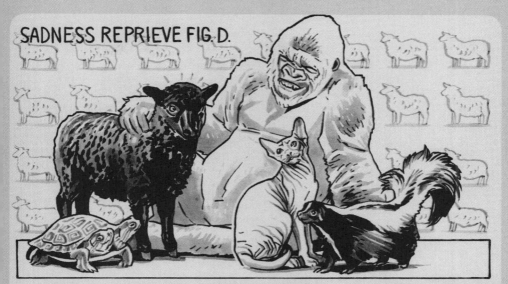

SADNESS REPRIEVE FIG. D.

FELLOW OUTCASTS EMBRACE HER UNIQUENESS AS A FEATURE, NOT A FLAW

TRAGEDY # 79

FANCY-PANTS ACADEMY STRUTS SUPERIORITY IN FRONT OF THE SCHOOL OF HARD KNOCKS

TRAGEDY # 80

LAZIEST LEMUR HAS EVEN
GROWN TIRED OF LYING AROUND

TRAGEDY #81

THE DISHES DON'T CARE WHOSE TURN IT IS;
THEY JUST WANT TO FEEL CLEAN AGAIN

TRAGEDY # 82

CASUAL ATTIRE IS FORBIDDEN AMONGST THE EMPERORS

TRAGEDY # 83

ANOTHER MEAL RUINED BY FAHRENHEIT V. CELSIUS

TRAGEDY # 84

WERE IT NOT FOR TIME, SPACE AND LANGUAGE
THESE THREE WOULD BE THE BEST OF FRIENDS

TRAGEDY # 85

YOU HAVE NO MONOCLE INSURANCE

BENJAMIN DEWEY

TRAGEDY #86

CONSTABLES CANNOT GET A STRAIGHT STORY FROM BABBLING BROOK

TRAGEDY #87

DISASTER IS THE SOLE OUTCOME OF MATCHMAKER'S EFFORTS

TRAGEDY# 88

HIPPO'S WIG COLLECTION MAKES
HIM A PRISONER OF POSSESSIONS

TRAGEDY# 89

PICKY MAGICIAN DISSATISFIED BY SOUP

BENJAMIN DEWEY

TRAGEDY # 90

THEY SUDDENLY APPEAR IN THE SKY, SHRIEKING UNSPEAKABLY

TRAGEDY#91

EITHER OAR BUT NOT BOTH

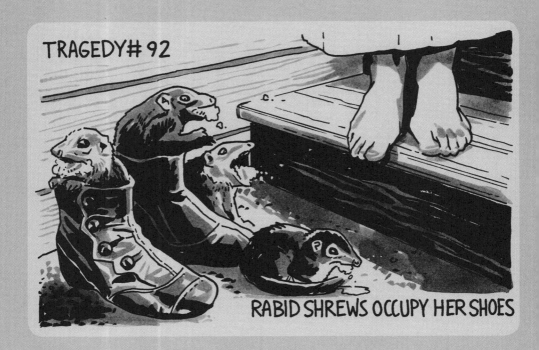

TRAGEDY# 92

RABID SHREWS OCCUPY HER SHOES

TRAGEDY# 93

PSYCHIC BEETLE'S DIRE WARNING WON'T
REACH THE PRESIDENT IN TIME

BENJAMIN DEWEY

TRAGEDY # 94

THOUGHTLESS PROGENY LEAVE HIM INSUFFICIENT SPACE TO ROLL OVER IN HIS GRAVE

TRAGEDY # 95

MISSING PET DOESN'T WANT TO BE FOUND

TRAGEDY # 96

AVOID KEEPING ALL YOUR VALUABLES IN ONE LOCATION

TRAGEDY # 97

MERMAIDS CANNOT REACH
THE DELICIOUS BLUEBERRIES

BENJAMIN DEWEY

HE'S OLD ENOUGH, HE HAS THE MONEY; THEY STILL WON'T SELL IT

SADNESS REPRIEVE FIG. E.

MIGHTY WARRIOR DISCOVERS ADVENTURES THAT DON'T REQUIRE HIS BLADE

TRAGEDY # 99

SOMEONE MIXED UP A WHOLE MESS OF OATMEAL IN THE OLD WELL

TRAGEDY # 100

A HUNDRED YEARS OF HICCUPS

BENJAMIN DEWEY

TRAGEDY #101

ALAS, THE VITAL PARCEL THEY AWAIT FELL INTO A RAVINE

TRAGEDY #102

SCARECROW'S DATE ACCEPTS OFFER TO BE WITH A 'REAL MAN'

TRAGEDY # 103

TIGERS TAKE THE ICE CREAM

TRAGEDY # 104

CONQUERED BY KUDZU

BENJAMIN DEWEY

TRAGEDY #105

INVINCIBLE, OMNIPRESENT & DISPARAGING BUTTERFLY

TRAGEDY #106

NOW EAGLE UNDERSTANDS; EVEN HIS OFT SUPERIOR VISION IS A MERE SLIVER OF THE ELECTROMAGNETIC SPECTRUM

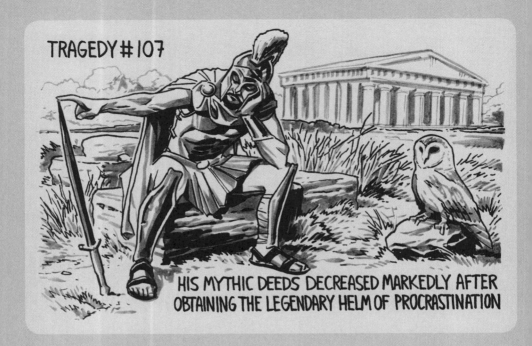

TRAGEDY #107

HIS MYTHIC DEEDS DECREASED MARKEDLY AFTER
OBTAINING THE LEGENDARY HELM OF PROCRASTINATION

TRAGEDY #108

WILD HORSES DECIDE TO TEST HIS CLAIM

BENJAMIN DEWEY

TRAGEDY #109

AMORPHOUS BLOB HAS NO REGARD FOR WAITING LIST

TRAGEDY #110

NO ONE IS BUYING LEMONADE

BALLOON RACE
MISHAP

TOSSED ABOUT, FOR SPORT, UPON THE OPEN SEA

BENJAMIN DEWEY

TRAGEDY #113 THE WOEFUL TALE OF LIL MEOWSKERS: PART III

MAROONED ON SLUDGE ISLAND

TRAGEDY #114 THE WOEFUL TALE OF LIL MEOWSKERS: PART IV

ENCIRCLED BY HOSTILE SLIME-PHANTOMS

TRAGEDY #115 THE WOEFUL TALE OF LIL MEOWSKERS: PART V

OFFERED UP TO THE BEHEMOTH

TRAGEDY #116: THE WOEFUL TALE OF LIL MEOWSKERS: PART VI

CAUGHT AMIDST LONG-STANDING FEUD

BENJAMIN DEWEY

HE FACED ALMOST-CERTAIN DOOM BUT LIVED TO TELL THE TALE

TRAGEDY #117

TRIBUTE SYMPHONY GOES TO WASTE;
THE ALL-SEEING EYE LACKS EARS

TRAGEDY #118

ALICORN BREAKAGE

BENJAMIN DEWEY

SADNESS REPRIEVE FIG. F.

'NATURE'S BANDITS' GIVE BACK

TRAGEDY #119

THE MUSK OX MOB
OWNS THE STREETS

TRAGEDY #120

SENTIMENTAL PROSPECTOR
CAN'T BEAR TO PART WITH
BABY-HEAD-SHAPED NUGGET

TRAGEDY #121

INHABITING TWO WORLDS; SOCIALLY AWKWARD IN BOTH

BENJAMIN DEWEY

TRAGEDY # 122

SUBSTANDARD ENUNCIATION
RESULTS IN 'FABULOUS WITCHES'

TRAGEDY # 123

THERE IS SUCH A THING AS TOO SPICY

TRAGEDY #124

TEAKETTLE ATTACK

TRAGEDY #125

BASHFUL STATUE HOLDS IN HER TEARS TILL IT RAINS

TRAGEDY #126

HE CAN SOAR ABOVE ANYTHING EXCEPT HIS PAST AT SEA

TRAGEDY #127

THE MAGMANAUTS DIDN'T HARVEST ENOUGH STALAGMITES TO APPEASE THE LAVA OVERLORD

TRAGEDY #128

A SLEW OF DIRTY-DISH DISCOVERIES SULLIES THE CLEAN-PLATE CLUB'S STERLING REPUTATION

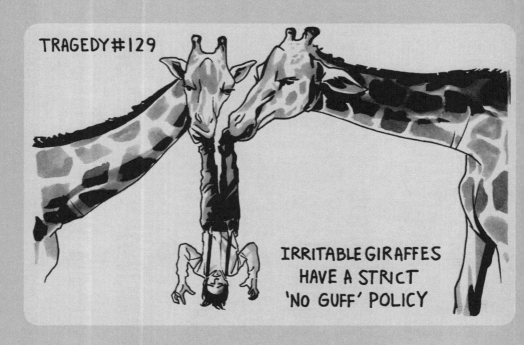

TRAGEDY #129

IRRITABLE GIRAFFES HAVE A STRICT 'NO GUFF' POLICY

BENJAMIN DEWEY

TRAGEDY #130

MEETING HIS HEROES WAS DISHEARTENING

TRAGEDY #131

WHEN YOU BUY BUDGET INVISIBILITY SERUM YOU GET WHAT YOU PAY FOR

TRAGEDY #132

AT THIS LATITUDE, THE WORST NIGHT OF YOUR LIFE CAN LAST FOR MONTHS

TRAGEDY #133

ORGAN-GRINDER-AND-MONKEY PARTNERSHIP PUBLICLY COLLAPSES

BENJAMIN DEWEY

TRAGEDY #134

HIS LOGIC WAS PRESERVED BUT HIS DANCE MOVES WERE SUPPRESSED

TRAGEDY #135

WORLD'S BEST CROWBAR SITS UNUSED

TRAGEDY #136

DOPPELGÄNGER INTERCEPTS AFFECTIONS INTENDED FOR YOU

TRAGEDY #137

SEA OTTERS READ YOUR DIARY
AND EAT YOUR LOVE LETTERS

BENJAMIN DEWEY

TRAGEDY # 138

FUTURE GENERATIONS WILL CONSIDER HIM A VISIONARY GENIUS

TRAGEDY # 139

FOLLOWING THE BOUNCING BALL WAS A BAD IDEA

SADNESS REPRIEVE FIG. G.

DIMETRODON TRANSMUTES BLUSTERY
EMBARRASSMENT INTO EXTREME INNOVATION

BENJAMIN DEWEY

TRAGEDY #140

COUNTING EACH OTHER DIDN'T WORK;
THE SHEEP CAN'T SLEEP

TRAGEDY #141

SPURNED ELEPHANT SEAL SEEKS REVENGE

TRAGEDY #142

OGRE MONOPOLIZES TEETER-TOTTER

TRAGEDY #143

THE NIGHT-COW FEASTS UPON THEIR SWEETEST DREAMS

BENJAMIN DEWEY

TRAGEDY #144

IN ALL THE MERRIMENT, LORD AND LADY BRAMBLESHIRE SPRAIN THEIR TEA FINGERS

TRAGEDY #145

AS TIME PASSED, SHE VISITED LESS & LESS

TRAGEDY #146

PARANOID PUGILISTS' ANNUAL PICNIC
YIELDS INEVITABLE FISTICUFFS FLURRY

TRAGEDY #147

ANTIDOTE NOT LABELED

BENJAMIN DEWEY

TRAGEDY # 148

MOTHS EAT THE ONLY MAP TO ATLANTIS

TRAGEDY # 149

THEY DEEMED IT 'STRIKING BUT NOT EXHIBIT WORTHY'

TRAGEDY # 150

ELDERLY DOG FLAT-OUT REFUSES TO TRY LEARNING ANY GNU TRICKS

TRAGEDY # 151

HE CAN SEE PARALLEL WORLDS; HE IS BETTER OFF IN ALL OF THEM

BENJAMIN DEWEY

TRAGEDY #152

MAGIC FOUNTAIN RESENTS CHARITY,
IGNORES ALL THE WISHES

TRAGEDY #153

NO CUPCAKES PERMITTED AT THE COTILLION

TRAGEDY #154

LOVING COUPLE'S VARMINTS DESPISE ONE ANOTHER

TRAGEDY # 155

CEREAL BARON
SUSPENDS ALL PRODUCTION

BENJAMIN DEWEY

TRAGEDY #156

TEENAGE PONY CLIQUE RAVAGED BY SCANDALOUS GOSSIP

TRAGEDY #157

IT WAS HER THING LONG BEFORE
IT BECAME THE LATEST THING

TRAGEDY # 158

PRODIGY PIGLET WINS THE SPELLING BEE
AND HIS PARENTS COULD NOT CARE LESS

SADNESS REPRIEVE FIG. H.

SQUIDS AT PLAY

BENJAMIN DEWEY

EACH OWNER OF THE GOLDEN PIPE
MEETS AN EARLY AND UNUSUAL END

TRAGEDY #160

THE IMPENETRABLE FORTRESS DENIES ACCESS
TO ALL, INCLUDING FUN TIMES AND CARE PACKAGES

TRAGEDY # 161

INCREASINGLY ABSURD STATUS-SYMBOL
UMBRELLAS IMPEDE MOVEMENT ON THE BOULEVARDS

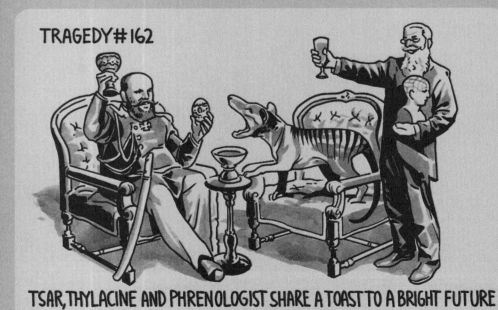

TRAGEDY # 162

TSAR, THYLACINE AND PHRENOLOGIST SHARE A TOAST TO A BRIGHT FUTURE

BENJAMIN DEWEY

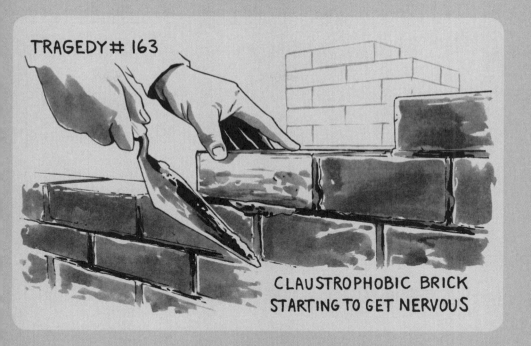

TRAGEDY # 163

CLAUSTROPHOBIC BRICK
STARTING TO GET NERVOUS

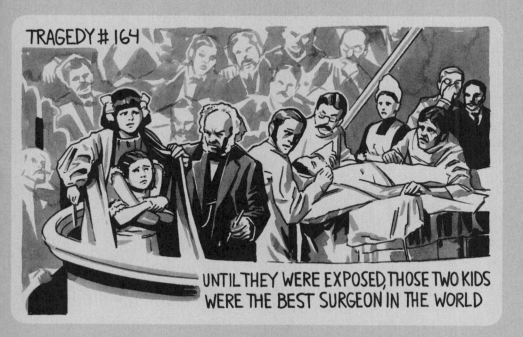

TRAGEDY # 164

UNTIL THEY WERE EXPOSED, THOSE TWO KIDS
WERE THE BEST SURGEON IN THE WORLD

TRAGEDY #165

PERSISTENT INSECT ACTUALLY HER LATE SWEETHEART REINCARNATED

TRAGEDY #166

HIS WORLD-PEACE MACHINE DID NOT IMPRESS WOMEN SO HE DISMANTLED IT

BENJAMIN DEWEY

TRAGEDY # 167

ANOTHER NAIVE MARSHAL FALLS FOR POSSUM PETE'S OLD RUSE

TRAGEDY # 168

IN HER SLUMBER, SHE CROSS STITCHES SHOCKINGLY FOUL THINGS

TRAGEDY # 169

GIANT-MONSTER CONVENTION
CONVENED IN YOUR VILLAGE

TRAGEDY # 170

CREATIVE CHAMELEON CAN BLEND IN
ANYWHERE EXCEPT WHERE HE GREW UP

BENJAMIN DEWEY

TRAGEDY # 171

THEY WERE REALLY LOOKING FORWARD TO PIE

TRAGEDY # 172

LUNGFISH FORECLOSURE

TRAGEDY # 173

THE ACCOUNT OF HIS PRIOR SHOPPING CONDUCT IS SIMPLE SLANDER

TRAGEDY # 174

SECRETARY OF PEGASUS PRESERVATION IS GROSSLY INCOMPETENT

BENJAMIN DEWEY

TRAGEDY #175

POLYMATH ANTEATER'S MANY OTHER ABILITIES GO UNACKNOWLEDGED

TRAGEDY #176

'STEW IN THE BATTLE-HORN' IS A GOOD PRANK
UNLESS BARBARIANS ARE CRESTING THE HILLS

TRAGEDY # 177

THOSE WHO JOINED THE SHADOWY ORGANIZATION TO ENGAGE IN SKULLDUGGERY WERE LET DOWN BLANDLY

TRAGEDY # 178

SLOTH DIPLOMACY FAILURE

TRAGEDY #179

SQUIRREL'S ANTHOLOGY OF MOON POEMS MAKES EVERYTHING ELSE SEEM TRITE

SADNESS REPRIEVE FIG. I.

HUMPTY'S LOVED ONES GLAD THEY SOUGHT SECOND OPINION FROM KING'S LADIES & MARES

TRAGEDY #180

SNUGGLE CUB NEEDS A CUDDLE

TRAGEDY #181

FOUR STUBBORNLY COURTEOUS DRIVERS REMAIN AT
CROSSROADS INDEFINITELY REFUSING RIGHT OF WAY

BENJAMIN DEWEY

TRAGEDY #182

DECADES OF TEACHING INDIFFERENT URCHINS LEAVES PROFESSOR SEAHORSE WEARY

TRAGEDY #183

THINGS THAT GO BUMP IN THE NIGHT HAVE NOTHING TO DO DURING THE DAY

TRAGEDY # 184

MOST MELANCHOLY GIRL
OUTDONE BY MORBID OSTRICH

TRAGEDY #185

ART ICON REVISITS HIS BELOVED EARLY
OEUVRE WITH EMBARRASSING ADDITIONS

BENJAMIN DEWEY

TRAGEDY #186

DO NOT INVITE PIXIES TO TEA

TRAGEDY #187

THE LIGHT AT THE END OF THE TUNNEL WAS A MURDEROUS ORB

TRAGEDY # 188

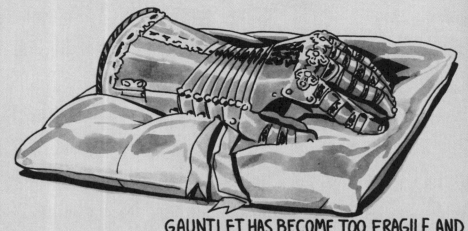

GAUNTLET HAS BECOME TOO FRAGILE AND
VALUABLE TO THROW DOWN ANYMORE

TRAGEDY # 189

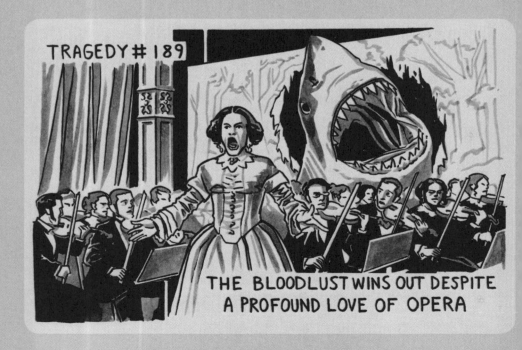

THE BLOODLUST WINS OUT DESPITE
A PROFOUND LOVE OF OPERA

BENJAMIN DEWEY

TRAGEDY #190

HE MADE IT ALMOST ALL THE WAY HOME WITHOUT DROPPING THEM

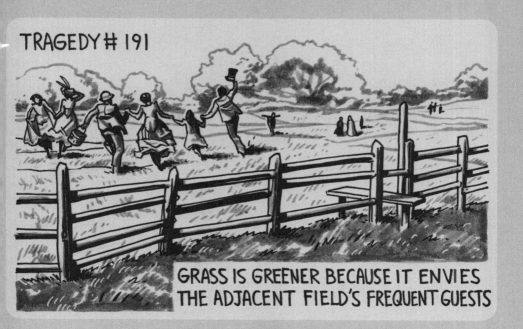

TRAGEDY #191

GRASS IS GREENER BECAUSE IT ENVIES
THE ADJACENT FIELD'S FREQUENT GUESTS

TRAGEDY #192

SHOW-AND-TELL TAKES
A HORRIFYING TURN

TRAGEDY #193

CENTAUR UNABLE TO
ATTEND TREEHOUSE BASH

BENJAMIN DEWEY

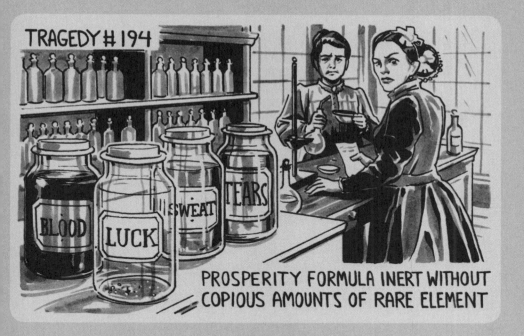

TRAGEDY #194

PROSPERITY FORMULA INERT WITHOUT COPIOUS AMOUNTS OF RARE ELEMENT

TRAGEDY #195

RESCUE TEAM'S DISGUISE NEARLY HAD THEM FOOLED

TRAGEDY # 196

HE WOULD LEAD THEM ON TO GLORIOUS ESCAPADES BUT THEY RESIST

TRAGEDY # 197

ZOMBIE BARBER CAN'T KEEP A JOB

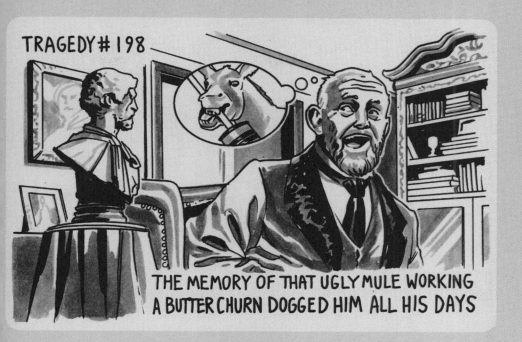

TRAGEDY #198

THE MEMORY OF THAT UGLY MULE WORKING A BUTTER CHURN DOGGED HIM ALL HIS DAYS

SADNESS REPRIEVE FIG. J.

TRAVEL-WEARY COMPASS FINALLY POINTED BACK TOWARD HOME

TRAGEDY #199

POLITE SOCIETY WAS BRISTLING WITH SCORN AFTER ONE WALTZ

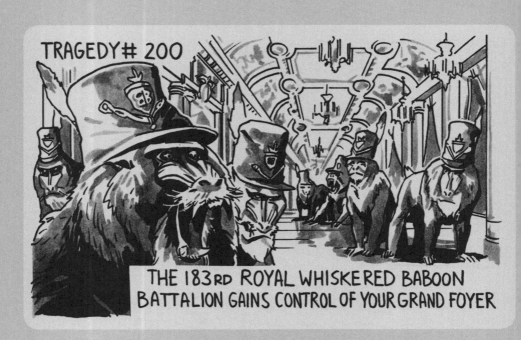

TRAGEDY #200

THE 183RD ROYAL WHISKERED BABOON BATTALION GAINS CONTROL OF YOUR GRAND FOYER

BENJAMIN DEWEY

TRAGEDY # 201

CHOCOLATE FACTORY
MELTDOWN

TRAGEDY # 202

THE GRANDIOSE GRAHAM CRACKER STACKS
HELD UP UNTIL THE BIRDS MIGRATED BACK

TRAGEDY # 203

THIS IS WHY WE CAN'T HAVE NICE THINGS

TRAGEDY # 204

GREAT THINKER'S BEAUTY OFTEN
OVERSHADOWS HER BRILLIANT WORK

TRAGEDY # 205

POOR OLD BUCKET-SHOES TURNED
AWAY FROM YET ANOTHER FANCY BISTRO

TRAGEDY # 206

HE SPENT HIS ENTIRE FORTUNE ON
PINWHEELS SIMPLY TO BE NEAR HER

TRAGEDY # 207

THE 'CRYING STUMP' ONLY
SEATS ONE AT A TIME

TRAGEDY # 208

THE KERNELS OF TRUTH MAKE IT PLAIN THAT
WOMEN CONSIDER HIM UNCOUTH AND SMELLY

BENJAMIN DEWEY

TRAGEDY # 209

WOLF AND PELICAN ARE
NO LONGER ON SPEAKING TERMS

TRAGEDY # 210

YOUR LANTERN LIGHT DRAWS OUT THE SEWER MUTANTS

TRAGEDY # 211

HE WAS ALWAYS TOO BUSY GAZING AT THE STARS TO WATCH HIS OWN BACK

TRAGEDY # 212

NO AMOUNT OF MASSAGING CAN WORK OUT THESE KNOTS

TRAGEDY # 213

LIZARDS WITH SCISSORS
TAKE TO THE STREETS

TRAGEDY # 214

TOP-NOTCH TOWN CRIER'S TURF OVERTAKEN BY SUBPAR SHOUTERS

TRAGEDY# 215

PARASITE MORE POPULAR THAN HOST

TRAGEDY# 216

MANIFESTING THE ECCENTRIC DREAM OF FUDGE-MANSION COST HIM EVERYTHING ELSE

TRAGEDY # 217

MICE MISPLACE THEIR NICEST DICE AMONGST THE RICE

TRAGEDY # 218

TOURISTS ARRIVE BEFORE HE COULD POST ALL THE WARNING SIGNS

SADNESS REPRIEVE FIG. K.

UNLIKELY BOND FORMED THROUGH A SHARED PASSION FOR ART

TRAGEDY # 219

DESERT COMBO CAN'T SEEM
TO GENERATE AN AUDIENCE

BENJAMIN DEWEY

TRAGEDY # 220

FANCY CHAIR WON'T LET YOU SLEEP IN

TRAGEDY # 221

HER UNCOUTH DISPLAY OF PRIVILEGE ENSURED NO FURTHER SOCIAL INVITATIONS

TRAGEDY # 222

FOOLISH RAGAMUFFINS CHALLENGE
HUNGRY LION TO A REMATCH

TRAGEDY # 223

HEFTY TOLLS RESULT IN LESS TRAFFIC ON THE HIGH ROAD

BENJAMIN DEWEY

TRAGEDY #224

COUPLE'S FIRST KISS FOILED BY RUDE ROOSTER

TRAGEDY #225

CORSET SCORPIONS

TRAGEDY # 226

MOLE MEN STEAL ALL THE CHEESE

TRAGEDY # 227

UNLIT LIGHTHOUSE AND WET SOCKS

BENJAMIN DEWEY

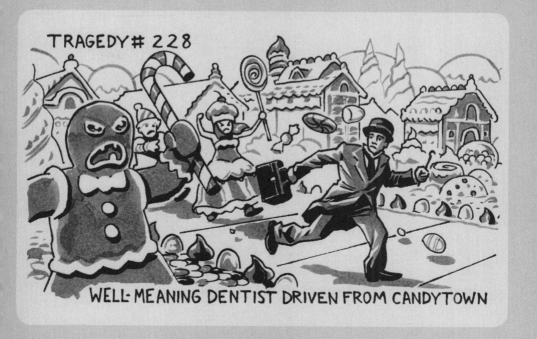

TRAGEDY # 228

WELL-MEANING DENTIST DRIVEN FROM CANDYTOWN

TRAGEDY # 229

THEY'RE GOOD ENOUGH TO KNOW HOW FAR THEY ARE FROM BEING THE BEST

BENJAMIN DEWEY

TRAGEDY # 232

FERTILITY MASKS ARE NOT PERMITTED IN THE CLASSROOM

TRAGEDY # 233

ARCHENEMIES DEVELOP INSEPARABLE BUDDY-WHISKERS

TRAGEDY # 234

ALL THE PRIME LURKING SPOTS ARE ALREADY TAKEN

TRAGEDY# 235

A NEW ROUND OF HIDE-AND-SEEK BEGINS WITHOUT ANY OF THEM LOOKING FOR HORSE

BENJAMIN DEWEY

TRAGEDY #236

SOULMATES, EACH ENGROSSED IN SAME TOME, NEVER MEET

TRAGEDY #237

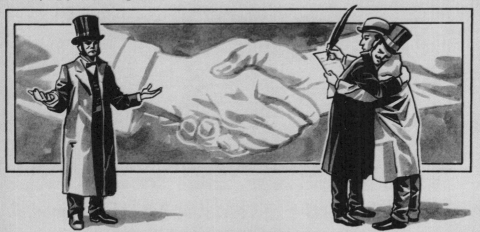

HANDSHAKE DEAL OVERRIDDEN BY HUGGING COMPACT

SADNESS REPRIEVE FIG. L.

SHALLOW FLIRTATION MATURES
INTO THE DEEPEST AFFECTION

BENJAMIN DEWEY

TRAGEDY # 238

KIWI THOUGHT THAT HE AND STRAWBERRY HAD SOMETHING SPECIAL

TRAGEDY # 239

ARRIVING TOO LATE FOR CAKE

TRAGEDY # 240

CAPYBARA'S BLANKET IS TRAPPED UNDER A ROCK

TRAGEDY # 241

COMB LOSES SEVERAL TEETH
DURING FIGHT WITH BRUSH

TRAGEDY #242

SHY SORCERER CAN ONLY PERFORM HIS FANTASTIC FEATS IN SOLITUDE

TRAGEDY #243

THEY TRIED TO PILFER HIS SCARF; NOW WE'RE ALL GOING TO PAY

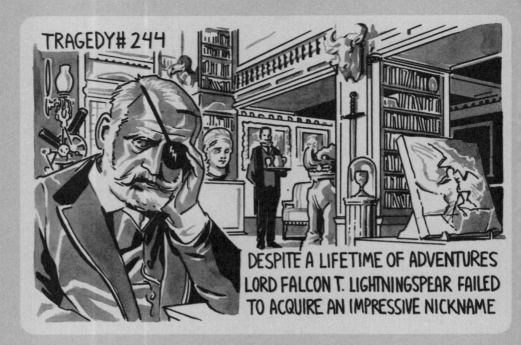

TRAGEDY # 244

DESPITE A LIFETIME OF ADVENTURES LORD FALCON T. LIGHTNINGSPEAR FAILED TO ACQUIRE AN IMPRESSIVE NICKNAME

TRAGEDY # 245

EARLY INVENTOR HITS HER SOPHOMORE SLUMP

BENJAMIN DEWEY

TRAGEDY # 246

LIFE GIVES LEMONS TO EVERYBODY BUT YOU

TRAGEDY # 247

GRANDFATHER CLOCK DISAPPOINTED BY DESCENDANTS

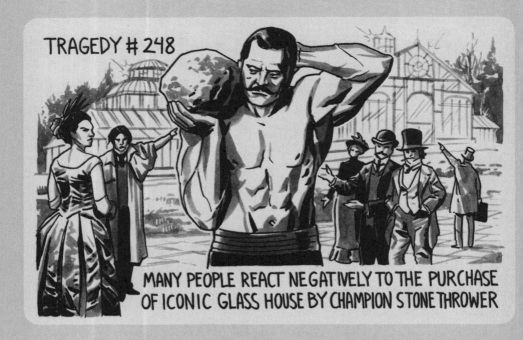

TRAGEDY #248

MANY PEOPLE REACT NEGATIVELY TO THE PURCHASE OF ICONIC GLASS HOUSE BY CHAMPION STONE THROWER

TRAGEDY #249

THEY WERE INSTRUCTED NOT TO OPEN THE BOX; SO WHY WAS IT LEFT WITH THEM?

BENJAMIN DEWEY

TRAGEDY # 250

KRAKEN ATTENDS
REGATTA GALA UNINVITED

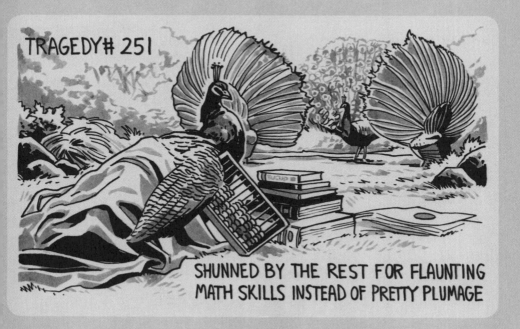

TRAGEDY# 251

SHUNNED BY THE REST FOR FLAUNTING
MATH SKILLS INSTEAD OF PRETTY PLUMAGE

TRAGEDY # 252

THE ORACLE HAS DISPENSED ADVICE FOR 10,000 YEARS; NOBODY EVER ASKS HOW SHE'S DOING

TRAGEDY# 253

POSEIDON DERAILS A SEASIDE PROPOSAL

BENJAMIN DEWEY

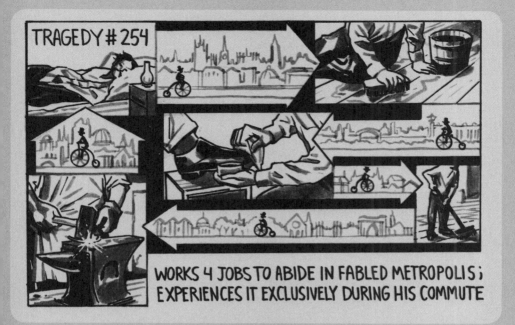

TRAGEDY # 254

WORKS 4 JOBS TO ABIDE IN FABLED METROPOLIS;
EXPERIENCES IT EXCLUSIVELY DURING HIS COMMUTE

TRAGEDY # 255

IGNORED BY HER OWN SPIRIT ANIMAL

TRAGEDY # 256

EVERY KITCHEN IS TOO
HOT FOR CHEF SNOWMAN

TRAGEDY # 257

JUST ONCE, HE WOULD LIKE TO WEAR
THEM WITHOUT SOMEONE COMMENTING

BENJAMIN DEWEY

TRAGEDY # 258

TIME MACHINE CRASH

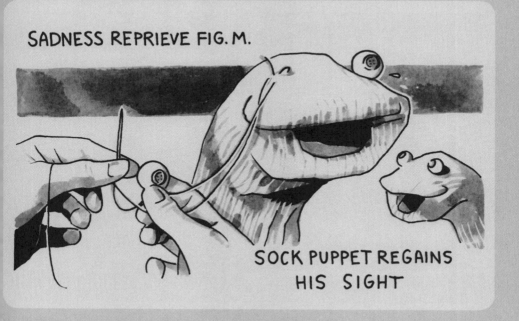

SADNESS REPRIEVE FIG. M.

SOCK PUPPET REGAINS
HIS SIGHT

TRAGEDY # 259

CYCLOPS CATCH

TRAGEDY # 260

'METAL ROD-HAT' DANCE FAD SHORT-LIVED

BENJAMIN DEWEY

TRAGEDY # 261

PTERODACTYL FRUSTRATES EVERY ATTEMPT AT PASTORAL PAINTING

TRAGEDY # 262

SELFISH CAT WITHHOLDS RECIPE FOR JOY

TRAGEDY # 263

HE'D THOUGHT IT WAS A BAD TOSS; THEN A LETTER CAME
DETAILING BOOMERANG'S REASONS FOR NOT RETURNING

TRAGEDY # 264

THE LAST DODO'S LOVE HAD HEALING POWERS; SO DID ITS MEAT

BENJAMIN DEWEY

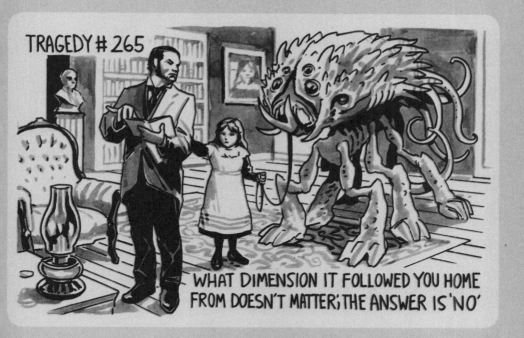

TRAGEDY # 265

WHAT DIMENSION IT FOLLOWED YOU HOME FROM DOESN'T MATTER; THE ANSWER IS 'NO'

TRAGEDY # 266

WHEN THE EMPIRE COLLAPSED, HIS SENSE OF PURPOSE WENT WITH IT

TRAGEDY # 267

NOT THE RIGHT KEYS

TRAGEDY # 268

SEEMINGLY IDYLLIC SWIMMING HOLE IS
THE ENTRANCE TO ABOMINATION'S LAIR

BENJAMIN DEWEY

TRAGEDY # 269

SLOW & STEADY BLOWS THE DEADLINE

TRAGEDY # 270

TAXIDERMIST AND NECROMANCER MAKE BAD ROOMMATES

TRAGEDY #271

NO ECHELON OF GLORY IS LOFTY ENOUGH TO ELICIT REVERENCE FROM THE PIGEON POPULACE

TRAGEDY #272

ONE HAMMERHEAD ON YOUR DOORSTEP MIGHT BE A FLUKE; THREE OF THEM IS A DARK OMEN

BENJAMIN DEWEY

TRAGEDY #273

EACH YEAR SINCE TURNING NINE HUNDRED & TWO, IMMORTAL GROUNDHOG HAS HARBORED A SINGLE WISH

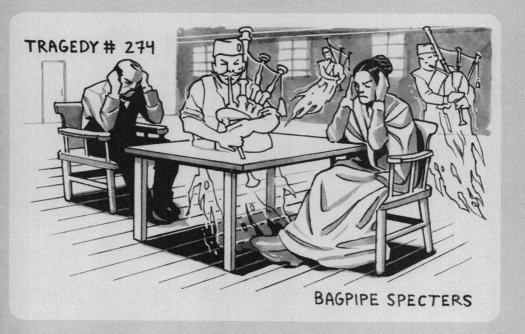

TRAGEDY #274

BAGPIPE SPECTERS

TRAGEDY # 275

SASSY YAKS LACK RESPECT FOR SACRED CIRCLE

TRAGEDY # 276

SHE REMAINS UNMOVED BY DIDGERIDOO SERENADE

BENJAMIN DEWEY

TRAGEDY # 277

THE THING UNDER THE BED HAS STARTED INVITING FRIENDS OVER

TRAGEDY # 278

HYPNOTIST HUSBAND & WIFE IRREVOCABLY TRIGGER EACH OTHER MID-SPAT

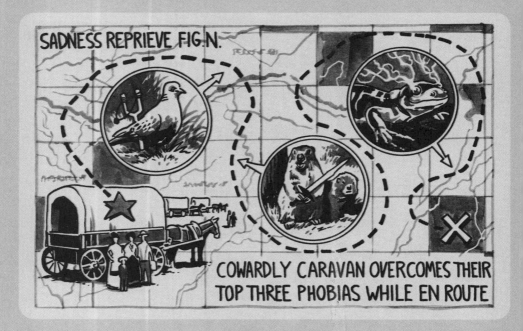

BENJAMIN DEWEY

TRAGEDY # 280

DON'T ROAST PEANUTS IN THE CROW'S NEST

TRAGEDY # 281

HARSH CRITIC USES BROOM TO EXPRESS HER DISAPPROVAL OF SPIDER'S LATEST WORK

TRAGEDY # 282

PANTHER-NINJA'S GIFT IS ALSO HIS CURSE;
NO ONE NOTICES HIM DURING PARTIES

TRAGEDY # 283

APPLES LEARN THE TRUTH ABOUT
LIFE BEYOND THE ORCHARD

BENJAMIN DEWEY

TRAGEDY # 284

PERFECTLY GOOD BOOT CAN'T RECALL HOW HE ENDED UP IN THE STREET WITHOUT A PARTNER

TRAGEDY # 285

SHE CAME TO THIS MOOR TO ENJOY THE GLOOM AND THEY ARE SPOILING IT

TRAGEDY # 286

RAPSCALLIONS ABSCOND IN YOUR DIRIGIBLE
WHILE YOU ARE ENJOYING PUDDING

TRAGEDY # 287

THE CANE WITH A BLADE IN IT IS STILL AT HOME

BENJAMIN DEWEY

TRAGEDY # 288

DRUNKEN ELEPHANT CRUSHED YOUR BED AGAIN

TRAGEDY # 289

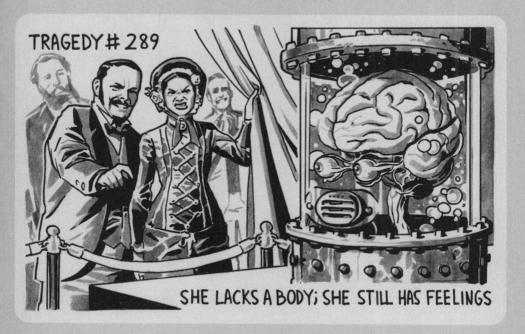

SHE LACKS A BODY; SHE STILL HAS FEELINGS

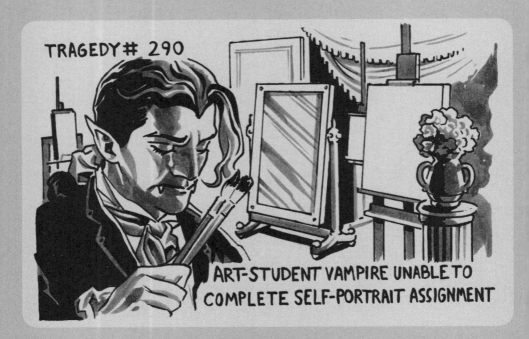

TRAGEDY # 290

ART-STUDENT VAMPIRE UNABLE TO COMPLETE SELF-PORTRAIT ASSIGNMENT

TRAGEDY # 291

SET UPON BY SALESMEN

164

BENJAMIN DEWEY

TRAGEDY # 292

HATTER-HABERDASHER STUMPED BY UNIQUE PATRON

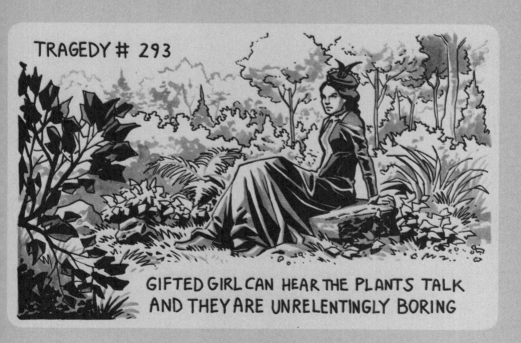

TRAGEDY # 293

GIFTED GIRL CAN HEAR THE PLANTS TALK AND THEY ARE UNRELENTINGLY BORING

TRAGEDY # 294

TITANIC TOAD
BLOCKS THE ROAD

TRAGEDY # 295

AIDED BY THE WIND, HER FAVORITE DRESS MAKES A BREAK FOR IT

BENJAMIN DEWEY

TRAGEDY# 296

VIGILANTE CHIMNEY SWEEP BEGINNING TO
LOSE FAITH IN THE FIGHT AGAINST CRIME AND SOOT

TRAGEDY# 297

DEFEATING HIS NEMESIS TAKES
THE ZEST OUT OF VILLAINY

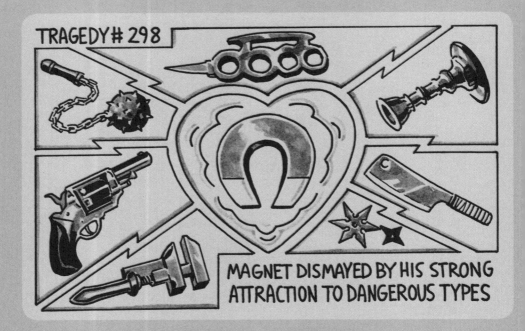

TRAGEDY # 298

MAGNET DISMAYED BY HIS STRONG ATTRACTION TO DANGEROUS TYPES

TRAGEDY # 299

CROWS WON'T GO

BENJAMIN DEWEY

TRAGEDY # 300

LLAMA DON'T ALLOW NO PRIVACY 'ROUND HERE

TRAGEDY # 301

ESTABLISHMENT ALREADY AT FULL CAPACITY OF ECCENTRIC PATRONS

BENJAMIN DEWEY

TRAGEDY # 302

MORTIFIED BY PARENTS' AFFECTIONS IN FRONT OF THE HORDE

TRAGEDY # 303

NOT A MIRAGE

TRAGEDY # 304

UPON ASKING IT BECAME EVIDENT THAT THIS AUDIENCE WAS, MOST DECIDEDLY, NOT READY TO ROCK

TRAGEDY # 305

FRIENDLY FLAG WAVES ALL DAY; NOBODY WAVES BACK

BENJAMIN DEWEY

TRAGEDY # 306

RHINO'S DAY JOB IS MAKING HIM BITTER

TRAGEDY # 307

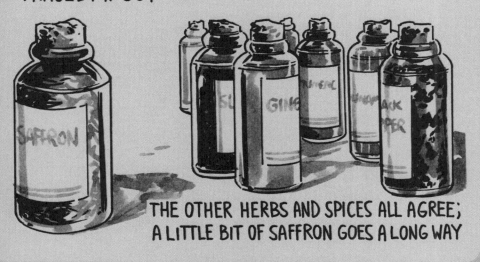

THE OTHER HERBS AND SPICES ALL AGREE;
A LITTLE BIT OF SAFFRON GOES A LONG WAY

TRAGEDY # 308

HER NEW PERFUME ATTRACTS CIRCUS FOLK

TRAGEDY#309

200 ANGRY WOMBATS WITH PARCELS TO SEND; 1 AVAILABLE CLERK

BENJAMIN DEWEY

TRAGEDY # 310

HE INTENDED TO PROTECT THE PUDDLE FROM HER CRUEL BOOTS

TRAGEDY # 311

THE TROLL RECEIVES YOUR PROMOTION

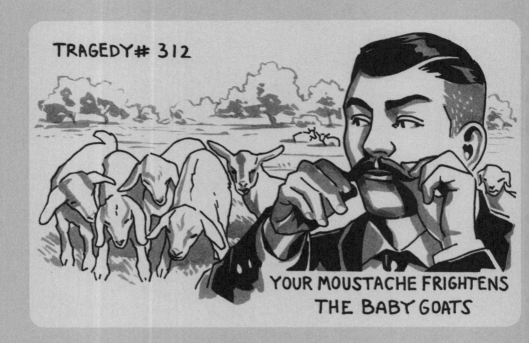

TRAGEDY # 312

YOUR MOUSTACHE FRIGHTENS
THE BABY GOATS

TRAGEDY # 313

THE RECENT APPEARANCE OF MASSIVE
CARNIVOROUS CABBAGES CONFIRMS THE CURSE

BENJAMIN DEWEY

TRAGEDY # 314

DEPOSED KING COBRAS
TURN TO A LIFE OF CRIME

TRAGEDY # 315

THE LINE TOOK SO LONG THAT THE
SEASON CHANGED WHILE THEY WAITED

TRAGEDY #316

OLD FIGUREHEAD STILL GETS SEASICK

TRAGEDY #317

GREATEST CREATION ESCAPED UNFINISHED

BENJAMIN DEWEY

TRAGEDY # 318

HE PUT TOO MUCH FAITH IN HIS LUCKY CHARM

SADNESS REPRIEVE FIG. P.

THE KINGDOM FLOURISHED UNDER A JUST AND COMPASSIONATE RULER

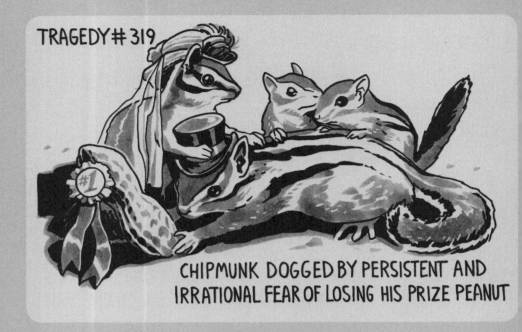

TRAGEDY # 319

CHIPMUNK DOGGED BY PERSISTENT AND
IRRATIONAL FEAR OF LOSING HIS PRIZE PEANUT

TRAGEDY # 320

BOILER-BOT NOT CONSTRUCTED TO KNOW LOVE

BENJAMIN DEWEY

TRAGEDY # 321

HOLDER OF THE SHORT STRAW MUST TELL
LORD URSUS THAT THERE'S NO MORE HONEY

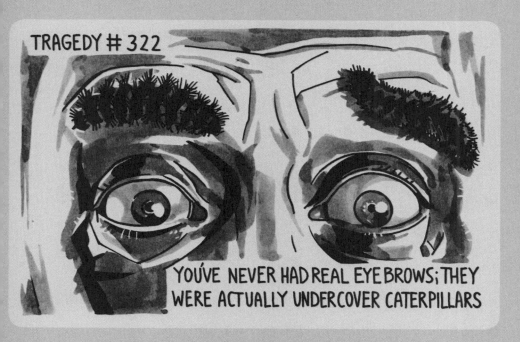

TRAGEDY # 322

YOU'VE NEVER HAD REAL EYEBROWS; THEY
WERE ACTUALLY UNDERCOVER CATERPILLARS

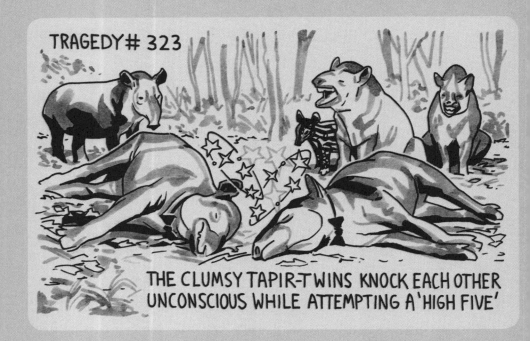

TRAGEDY # 323

THE CLUMSY TAPIR-TWINS KNOCK EACH OTHER UNCONSCIOUS WHILE ATTEMPTING A 'HIGH FIVE'

TRAGEDY # 324

SUAVE MUMMY'S PERFECT DATE ABOUT TO UNRAVEL

BENJAMIN DEWEY

TRAGEDY #325

CLOWN'S EXISTENTIAL CRISIS HITS MOMENTS BEFORE PIVOTAL PERFORMANCE

TRAGEDY #326

ETIQUETTE-OBSESSED BRONCO INCENSED BY INCORRECT FORMAL TABLE SETTINGS

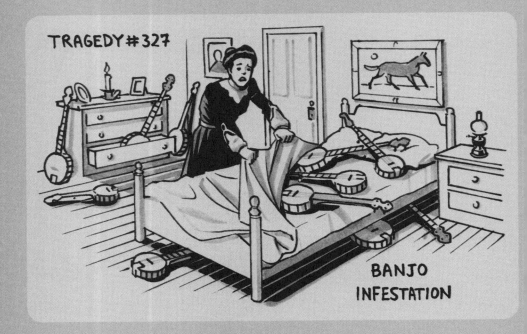

TRAGEDY #327

BANJO INFESTATION

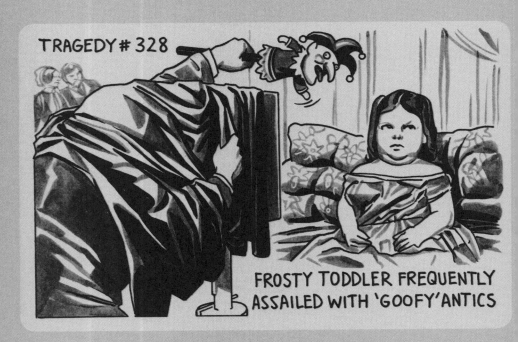

TRAGEDY #328

FROSTY TODDLER FREQUENTLY ASSAILED WITH 'GOOFY' ANTICS

BENJAMIN DEWEY

TRAGEDY # 329

YOUR TURNCOAT PARROT
LEADS ANOTHER MUTINY

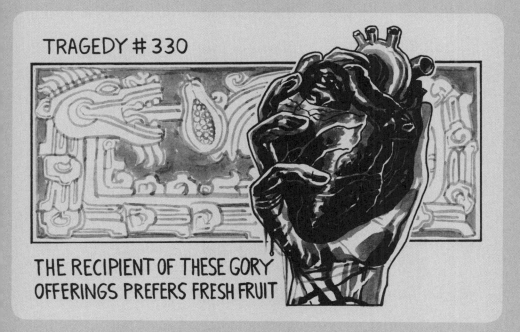

TRAGEDY # 330

THE RECIPIENT OF THESE GORY
OFFERINGS PREFERS FRESH FRUIT

TRAGEDY # 331

YOUR IMAGINARY FRIEND HOLDS YOU ACCOUNTABLE
FOR HER LACK OF INTERESTING QUALITIES

TRAGEDY # 332

STINGY BRIDGE KEEPER MUST HAVE HIS TOLL:
NO EXCEPTIONS FOR CHIVALROUS EXPLOITS

BENJAMIN DEWEY

TRAGEDY # 333

THE GIANT CENTIPEDE FROM UPSTAIRS BOUGHT TAP SHOES

TRAGEDY # 334

PEOPLE DON'T TAKE SHERIFF PUPPY SERIOUSLY

TRAGEDY # 335

ADOLESCENT DRAGON CLAIMS YOUR WHEELBARROW

TRAGEDY # 336

APATHETIC MESSENGER BIRD NEGLECTS TO DELIVER ARMISTICE AGREEMENT

BENJAMIN DEWEY

TRAGEDY # 337

IT'S A RAINY DAY IN BOTH REALMS

TRAGEDY # 338

IVORY TOWER INHABITANTS REQUIRE A
RESUPPLY FROM THOSE THEY'VE RIDICULED

SADNESS REPRIEVE FIG. Q

GREGARIOUS GEESE FLY IN FRIENDLY FORMATION

TRAGEDY # 339

STARFISH CAN REGROW A LOST LIMB
BUT NOT MEND HER BROKEN HEART

BENJAMIN DEWEY

TRAGEDY #340

POTATO PYRAMID LESS ASTOUNDING THAN PROMISED

TRAGEDY #341

THE OTHER TITANS REFUSE TO COVER FOR ATLAS SO HE NEVER GETS A TURN

TRAGEDY # 342

MOSS-BEAST HAS NO HELP BUILDING FUN-FORT

TRAGEDY # 343

HIGH-WIRE BREAKUP

BENJAMIN DEWEY

TRAGEDY # 344

BITTERLY BANNED MASCOT RETURNS
TO RUIN CHAMPIONSHIP MATCH

TRAGEDY # 345

INEPT 'STEAM·SQUAD' GIVEN CREDIT FOR
SELFLESS SUPER-FLEA'S VARIED VICTORIES

TRAGEDY # 346

HER HAIR COULD NOT BE TAMED SO SHE WAS FORCED TO SET IT FREE

TRAGEDY # 347

IT'S HARDER TO SHRUG IT OFF WHEN THEY SAY IT ABOUT YOUR MUSICIANSHIP

TRAGEDY # 348

ROCKET PRIVILEGES
REVOKED AS PUNISHMENT FOR
FRIDAY NIGHT SHENANIGANS

TRAGEDY# 349

EMERGENCY TURTLE DEPLORES WILLFUL RISK-TAKERS

TRAGEDY # 350

A MODEST KERFUFFLE
DESCENDS INTO WILD FOOFARAW

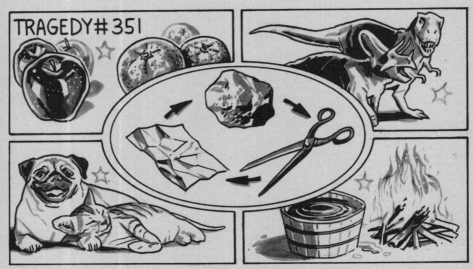

TRAGEDY # 351

FAMOUS TRIO CAPABLE OF RESOLVING ANY DISPUTE BUT THEIR OWN

BENJAMIN DEWEY

TRAGEDY # 352

THERE IS NO MUFFIN-BASKET LAVISH ENOUGH TO EXCUSE HIS BEHAVIOR AT HER SISTER'S GARDEN PARTY

TRAGEDY # 353

PANCAKES FORETELL YOUR DOWNFALL

TRAGEDY # 354

THEY SHOULD HAVE KNOWN THAT
THE SHED WOULDN'T HOLD IT

TRAGEDY # 355

VANILLA DISCOVERS THE NATURE
OF PUBLIC OPINION

BENJAMIN DEWEY

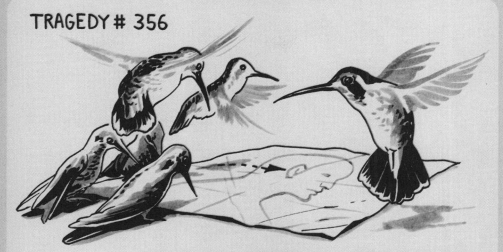

TRAGEDY # 356

ROGUE HUMMINGBIRDS DEVISE A PLAN TO
SUP UPON FRESH HUMAN BRAINS

TRAGEDY # 357

ONE OF THE SO-CALLED 'PERFECT SOLIDS' CAUGHT CHEATING

TRAGEDY # 358

THEY'VE STOLEN THE SHOES THAT GO BEST WITH HER NEW BOW

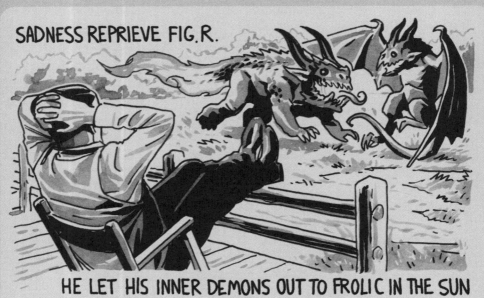

SADNESS REPRIEVE FIG. R.

HE LET HIS INNER DEMONS OUT TO FROLIC IN THE SUN

BENJAMIN DEWEY

TRAGEDY #359

THEIR CHOICE OF PINEAPPLES IN PLACE
OF PISTOLS ONLY MADE THE DUEL WORSE

TRAGEDY #360

THE FLOATING CITY IS REAL; IT'S POPULATED BY LITTERBUGS

TRAGEDY #361

PLATYPUS PERTURBED BY PLATITUDES

TRAGEDY #362

CAPTURING A PHOTOGRAPH OF THE COMPLETE MENAGERIE PROVES UNTENABLE

BENJAMIN DEWEY

TRAGEDY # 363

TRICERATOPS NEVER GOT
TO SEE THE OCEAN

TRAGEDY # 364

SIX DEGREES OF SEPARATION WAS NOT ENOUGH

TRAGEDY #365

HE QUICKLY RUED HIS OATH TO 'LIVE AS ONE OF THEM'

TRAGEDY #366

EVERYONE FORGOT ALLIGATOR'S BIRTHDAY

BENJAMIN DEWEY

TRAGEDY # 367

EXCLUSIVE SPOON-ROOM EXCLUDES BRUTES, HUGE NEWTS AND PRUNES

TRAGEDY # 368

FLYING CARPET WON'T BE TAMED

TRAGEDY # 369

FINAL WORDS OBSCURED BY CARROT-CRUNCHING LOUT

TRAGEDY # 370

DOLPHIN'S GIRLFRIEND LIKED HIM
BETTER WITH A BEARD

BENJAMIN DEWEY

TRAGEDY #371

ONGOING EGGPLANT EFFRONTERY

TRAGEDY #372

REPRESSED FEARS CT

MEMORY LN

TRIP DOWN MEMORY LANE GOES AWRY

TRAGEDY # 373

TICKET HOLDERS AT 'ECTOPLASM EXPLOSION' WERE THRILLED; THE CUSTODIAN WAS NOT

TRAGEDY # 374

CHUPACABRA'S MYTHICAL STATUS AND PHILOSOPHY DEGREE HINDER JOB PROSPECTS

BENJAMIN DEWEY

TRAGEDY # 375

BADGER BOTHERED AND BAFFLED BY OWL'S BASELESS RENOWN AS THE WISEST IN THE WOODS

TRAGEDY # 376

THEY SAID IT WOULD NEVER FLY; THEY WERE RIGHT

TRAGEDY # 377

CRYSTAL BALL OFFERS ONLY INSULTS

TRAGEDY # 378

JUMP ROPE OBSESSION PROMPTS BUREAUCRATIC BREAKDOWN

BENJAMIN DEWEY

SADNESS REPRIEVE FIG. S.

MASSIVE OFFERING OF MILK, FLOUR, COCOA, EGGS & SUGAR PRODUCES BROWNIE ERUPTION

TRAGEDY # 379

UP TILL THIS POINT IT HAD BEEN A SPLENDID HONEYMOON

TRAGEDY # 380

SHE'S SICK OF LOOKING AT HIS UGLY MUG

TRAGEDY # 381

SEAGULL UNWITTINGLY TAUNTS THE BARNACLES VIA TALES OF TRAVEL

BENJAMIN DEWEY

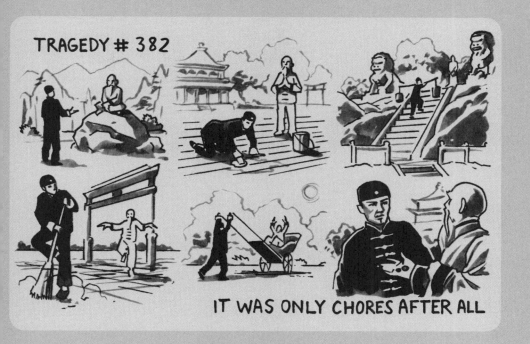

TRAGEDY # 382

IT WAS ONLY CHORES AFTER ALL

TRAGEDY # 383

ROUGH STONES DON'T GET SKIPPED

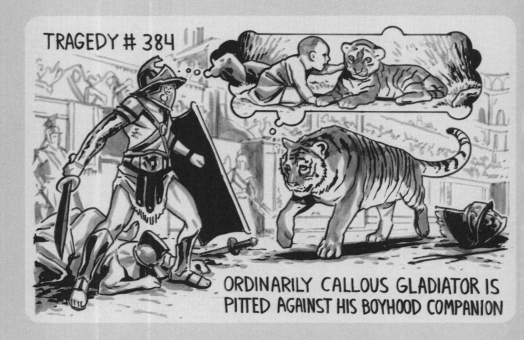

TRAGEDY # 384

ORDINARILY CALLOUS GLADIATOR IS PITTED AGAINST HIS BOYHOOD COMPANION

TRAGEDY # 385

PERIPHERAL VISIONS

BENJAMIN DEWEY

TRAGEDY # 386

'GOD-GIVEN' TALENT NOT RELEVANT IN HER LIFETIME

TRAGEDY # 387

CARRIED AWAY BY IMAGINATION

TRAGEDY # 388

WOLFMAN WON'T GET TO FINISH HIS NOVEL

TRAGEDY# 389

LITTLE PANGOLIN SINGS TOO SOFTLY
TO BE HEARD IN THE JUNGLE CHOIR

BENJAMIN DEWEY

TRAGEDY # 390

COUNT COOKIE-POCKETS PAINFULLY AWARE OF WHAT MAINTAINS HIS ENTOURAGE

TRAGEDY # 391

CURMUDGEON'S QUIET SUNDAY PLANS THWARTED BY JUBILATION

TRAGEDY #392

LAUNDRY PILE ACHIEVES SENTIENCE
SHORTLY BEFORE BEING DROWNED

TRAGEDY # 393

CRUNDLETON MANOR IS AWASH IN PYTHONS

BENJAMIN DEWEY

TRAGEDY #394

SHE STICKS TO THE SHADOWS

TRAGEDY #395

MIGHTY STAG'S GUTTURAL BELLOWING
SPOILS OPENING NIGHT

TRAGEDY #396

DEAD HORSE BEATS YOU

TRAGEDY #397

THE TREASURE HE HAD SOUGHT FOR SO LONG IS LITERALLY ANOTHER MAN'S TRASH

BENJAMIN DEWEY

TRAGEDY # 398

SPRING HAS SPRUNG

SADNESS REPRIEVE FIG. T.

LEOPARD FINDS IT SURPRISINGLY EASY
TO CHANGE HER SPOTS

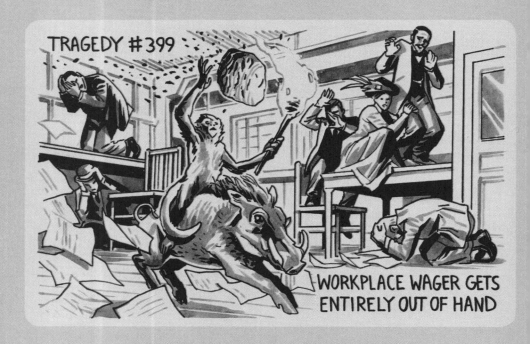

TRAGEDY #399

WORKPLACE WAGER GETS ENTIRELY OUT OF HAND

TRAGEDY #400

NOTORIOUS PIÑATA POSSE ESCAPES JUSTICE

TRAGEDY # 401

GENTLEMEN!

THEY'VE CUT THE FUNDS AND CALLED THE EXPEDITION BACK.

PITY.

BLAST.

ZOUNDS.

A MERE 200 MORE YARDS & EVERYONE COULD'VE SHARED EARTH'S CANDY CORE.

WE ALL VERY NEARLY RECIEVED A FREE & UNLIMITED TREAT SUPPLY

TRAGEDY # 402

AN AWKWARD OVERLAP BETWEEN PROFESSION AND SOCIAL CIRCLE

TRAGEDY #403

DOWNWARD-SPIRAL STAIRCASE

BENJAMIN DEWEY

TRAGEDY #404

WHILE SHE WAS OFF ACQUIRING RICHES, RAGS BECAME HUGELY POPULAR

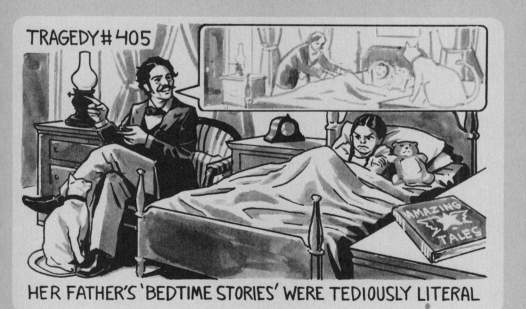

TRAGEDY #405

HER FATHER'S 'BEDTIME STORIES' WERE TEDIOUSLY LITERAL

TRAGEDY # 406

THE CAMP IS UNAWARE THAT THIS CHARMING DANCE IS A PRELUDE TO A GRIZZLY FEAST

TRAGEDY # 407

PROGNOSTICATOR - PORCUPINES PROTECT THEIR PERFECT PREDICTIONS FROM PUBLIC PRYING

BENJAMIN DEWEY

TRAGEDY#4O8

LATELY HER TRAINS OF THOUGHT ARE SUBJECT TO DELAYS & DERAILING

TRAGEDY#409

THEY SHOULD'VE ASKED ABOUT THE CARGO;
THEY SHOULDN'T HAVE TAKEN THE SHORTCUT

TRAGEDY # 410

THERE'S MORE THAN JUST GLASS BETWEEN
WINDOW WASHER AND THE GOOD LIFE

TRAGEDY # 411

HIGHER PRIMATE GIVEN LOWER SCORES

BENJAMIN DEWEY

TRAGEDY #412

CLAIRVOYANT GOBBLER SEES WHICH ANIMALS HUMANS HAVE EATEN

TRAGEDY #413

TOOTH FAIRY MUCH MORE AGGRESSIVE ABOUT COLLECTING FROM SENIORS

TRAGEDY # 414

SIDE KICK ORDERED TO HAND OVER AN ENCHANTED RING THAT COULD MAKE HIM A HERO

TRAGEDY # 415

PREJUDICE PREVENTS TWO OF THEM FROM TRUSTING THE INSPECTOR'S ADVICE

BENJAMIN DEWEY

SADNESS REPRIEVE FIG. U.

TUMBLEWEED TRANSCENDS HER ROOTS AND ROAMS THE WORLD

TRAGEDY # 416

KINDLY SERPENT'S APPLE CART
DOES POORLY IN PIOUS PART OF TOWN

TRAGEDY #417

QUEEN'S INNER CIRCLE INFILTRATED BY INCOGNITO PIRATE PRINCESS

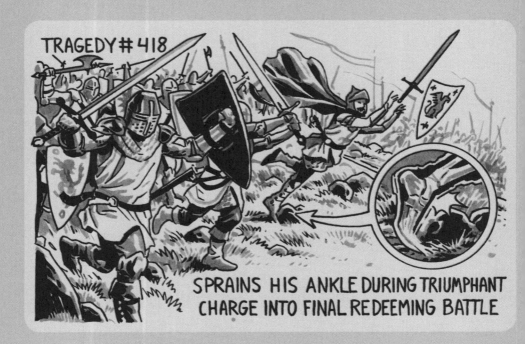

TRAGEDY #418

SPRAINS HIS ANKLE DURING TRIUMPHANT CHARGE INTO FINAL REDEEMING BATTLE

BENJAMIN DEWEY

TRAGEDY #419

CHANGE COMES FROM WITHIN

TRAGEDY #420

UNEXPECTED MEGAFAUNA RESURGENCE EXACERBATES ALREADY CROWDED PUBLIC TRANSPORT CONDITIONS

TRAGEDY # 421

WHISTLING WHILE HE WORKED AWOKE ANCIENT EVIL

TRAGEDY # 422

THEY ALWAYS STICK HER WITH THE CLEANING

BENJAMIN DEWEY

TRAGEDY#423

DASHING STRANGER IS REALLY A CREW
OF RATS IN AN ELABORATE GETUP

TRAGEDY#424

TOO BIG FOR SMALL TALK

TRAGEDY # 425

BETRAYED BY ONE OF THEIR OWN

BENJAMIN DEWEY

TRAGEDY # 426

HIBERNATION & MIGRATION CYCLES STIFLE THE POTENTIAL OF AN AMAZING ARCTIC BAND

TRAGEDY # 427

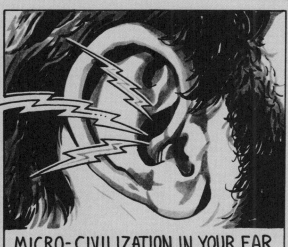

MICRO-CIVILIZATION IN YOUR EAR MARKS RECORD WAX HARVEST WITH INCESSANT BELL RINGING

TRAGEDY #428

AFFLUENCE ELIXIR HAS A SERIOUS SIDE EFFECT:
'INCREASED APPEAL TO APEX PREDATORS'

TRAGEDY #429

LADY'S LOCKET CONTENT
DOESN'T BODE WELL
FOR SNOOPING SUITOR

BENJAMIN DEWEY

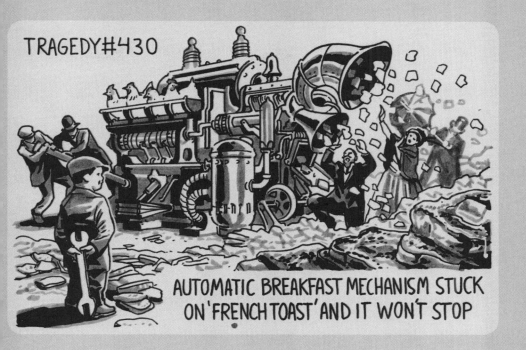

TRAGEDY #430

AUTOMATIC BREAKFAST MECHANISM STUCK ON 'FRENCH TOAST' AND IT WON'T STOP

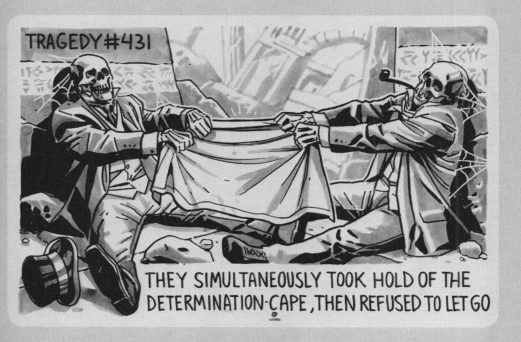

TRAGEDY #431

THEY SIMULTANEOUSLY TOOK HOLD OF THE DETERMINATION-CAPE, THEN REFUSED TO LET GO

TRAGEDY #432

EVEN THEIR DEADLIEST DARES ARE INEXPLICABLY IRRESISTIBLE

TRAGEDY #433

QUICK TRIP TO THE SHOP
BECOMES A TEST OF PATIENCE

BENJAMIN DEWEY

TRAGEDY #434

PUSHY POLTERGEIST INSISTENT ON THE EXCLUSIVE CONSUMPTION OF LEAFY GREENS

TRAGEDY #435

MANY DELIGHT IN THEIR FALLING AND SOME KICK THEM ONCE THEY'RE DOWN

TRAGEDY #436

'NICE FARM IN THE COUNTRY' AT CAPACITY

TRAGEDY #437

ONCE THE CREATIVE JUICES STARTED FLOWING, THEY WOULDN'T STOP

BENJAMIN DEWEY

TRAGEDY #438

THE CAT'S GOT HIS TONGUE¡
IT'LL COST AN ARM & A LEG TO BUY IT BACK

TRAGEDY #439

SHE CANNOT JOIN THE OTHERS
WITHOUT IDENTIFYING WHAT
PARTICULARLY FLOATS HER BOAT

TRAGEDY #440

HEALTH-CONSCIOUS GUARDIAN ANGELS 'SAVE' YOU FROM EVERY DIETARY THREAT

SADNESS REPRIEVE FIG. V.)

DOUGHY JOEY'S FORTUNE REFUTES THOSE WHO'D DISMISSED HIS BUSINESS IDEAS AS 'HALF-BAKED'

BENJAMIN DEWEY

TRAGEDY # 441

ONE IN EVERY TEN BARRELS OF THEM
IS ABSOLUTELY NO FUN WHATSOEVER

TRAGEDY #442

INTREPID DELIVERY MAN LEARNS THE HARD WAY;
THE MONKS 'CARE NOT FOR MATERIAL THINGS'

TRAGEDY #443

...AND SOME ARE DESTINED FOR GROSSNESS

BENJAMIN DEWEY

TRAGEDY #444

STOIC SENTINEL OBLIGED TO IGNORE IMPROBABLE FRIENDSHIPS WHILE ON DUTY

TRAGEDY #445

WORRY-WARTHOG'S CHIEF HOBBY IS TALKING HERSELF OUT OF ACTIVITIES

TRAGEDY #446

SPILLING THE MAGIC BEANS

BENJAMIN DEWEY

TRAGEDY #447

THE CRYSTAL KING & MADAM HAMMER-FINGERS
FACE A SERIOUS RELATIONSHIP IMPEDIMENT

TRAGEDY #448

COLONEL STINGFRIED RAYMOND FITZ-HUME THE SIXTH
IS INSULTED THAT ALL OF YOU INSIST ON SHORTENING HIS NAME

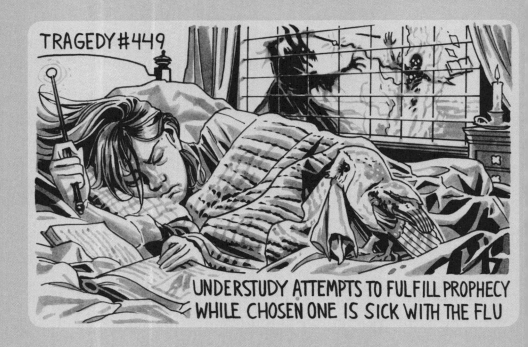

TRAGEDY #449

UNDERSTUDY ATTEMPTS TO FULFILL PROPHECY
WHILE CHOSEN ONE IS SICK WITH THE FLU

SADNESS REPRIEVE FIG.W

GAVEL'S FAMILY DOESN'T UNDERSTAND THE NATURE
OF HIS WORK BUT THEY'RE PROUD OF HIS SUCCESS

BENJAMIN DEWEY

TRAGEDY #450

STRONGMAN UNABLE TO LIFT
HIS BELOVED'S HEAVY HEART

TRAGEDY #451

DESPITE HIS VIGILANCE, THESE NOSE HARES KEEP REAPPEARING IN GREATER NUMBERS

TRAGEDY #452

PESSIMISTIC RECLUSE DRIVES AWAY BLESSINGS IN DISGUISE

BENJAMIN DEWEY

TRAGEDY #453

ELUSIVE CRYPTID HAS A POWERFUL ALLERGIC REACTION TO PHOTOGRAPHY

TRAGEDY #454

MARKETPLACE OF IDEAS OUT OF GOOD JUDGMENT;
THEY STILL HAD PLENTY OF RECKLESSNESS

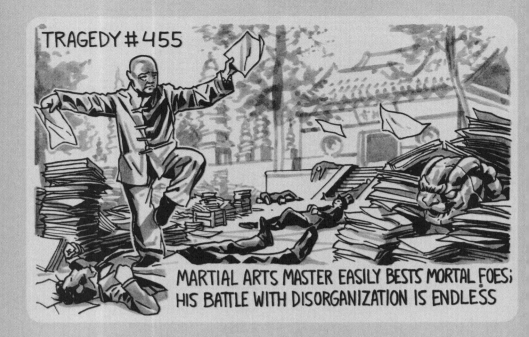

TRAGEDY #455

MARTIAL ARTS MASTER EASILY BESTS MORTAL FOES;
HIS BATTLE WITH DISORGANIZATION IS ENDLESS

TRAGEDY #456

THE SWALLOWS RETURN ANNUALLY;
'SLAUGHTER-MAW THE DEVOURER' REAPPEARS EVERY 500 YEARS

BENJAMIN DEWEY

TRAGEDY #457

FORTUNE-TATTLER GETS YOU PREEMPTIVELY IMPRISONED

SADNESS REPRIEVE FIG. X

THE EARLY BIRD AND THE WORM 'GET' EACH OTHER

TRAGEDY # 458

FAULTY DOWSING ROD LEADS TO A SUCCESSION OF WATERY GRAVES

BENJAMIN DEWEY

TRAGEDY #459

SLEEPWALKING SHUT-IN OBLIVIOUS OF HER OWN RISKY STUNTS

TRAGEDY #460

AT TIMES, THE TRUE KING OF THE JUNGLE IS 'DEPRESSION'

CENSOR-LOCUSTS

SADNESS REPRIEVE FIG. Y.

MINOTAUR QUITS MAZE WORK
TO PRACTICE THE CELLO

BENJAMIN DEWEY

TRAGEDY #463

HER FRIENDSHIP WITH THE OLD SYCAMORE WAS TRAGICALLY CUT SHORT

TRAGEDY #464

EXPEDITION TO THE 'SWITCHEROO'NIVERSE' INCURS APT SIDE EFFECT

BENJAMIN DEWEY

TRAGEDY #465

BOTTLE'S MESSAGE EXPLICITLY STATES THAT IT'S NOT FOR HER

TRAGEDY #466

WEASEL OPTS FOR SNOOZE IN HANDBASKET, IGNORANT OF ITS FINAL DESTINATION

TRAGEDY # 467

HE WAS FINALLY WELCOME AT THE CLUB; HIS HORNET'S NESTS WERE NOT

TRAGEDY #468

THEIR BARK & BITE ARE BOTH MODEST
DANGERS COMPARED WITH THE FIREBALLS

BENJAMIN DEWEY

TRAGEDY #469

HAVING IT AND EATING IT TOO IS GEOMETRICALLY IMPOSSIBLE

TRAGEDY #470

HOMICIDAL DOE ESCAPES CONVICTION BY DUPING GULLIBLE JURY

TRAGEDY #471

CHILD ADVENTURER WAVES OFF HEALING SPRITES
HE INCORRECTLY IDENTIFIES AS 'COOTIES'

TRAGEDY #472

SUPPLY CHAIN BREAKS BECAUSE OF WEAK LYNX

TRAGEDY #473

HUGE & AFFABLE 'FIREMEN' TREATED HARSHLY BY THEIR HUMAN NAMESAKES

TRAGEDY #474

LIGHTNING IN A BOTTLE
GOES UNDERUTILIZED

TRAGEDY #475

DISGRUNTLED GARDENER LETS THE TOPIARY DO THE TALKING

TRAGEDY #476

ASTRONOMER PIRANHA MARGINALIZED FOR SUGGESTING THERE'S SOMETHING GREATER THAN SKELETONIZING

BENJAMIN DEWEY

TRAGEDY #477

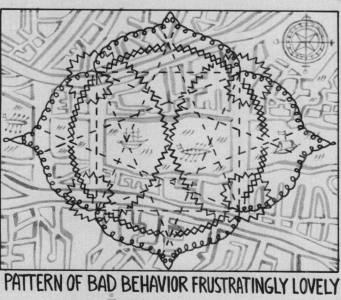

PATTERN OF BAD BEHAVIOR FRUSTRATINGLY LOVELY

TRAGEDY #478

'HYENA & SONS: UNDERTAKERS' DIDN'T LAST LONG

TRAGEDY # 479

ONE HAND, RESENTFULLY, WASHES THE OTHER

TRAGEDY # 480

HE SAVES UP FOR MONTHS; THEY DON'T ACCEPT SAND DOLLARS

BENJAMIN DEWEY

TRAGEDY #481

'DRESSING FOR THE JOB YOU WANT' CAN TOTALLY BACKFIRE

TRAGEDY #482

CAT-LADY & LADY-CAT RECEIVE WILDLY DIFFERENT RECEPTIONS

TRAGEDY #483

OLD KNEES' WEATHER FORECASTING INCREASINGLY CONTRADICTORY

TRAGEDY #484

'TAKING A CLOSER LOOK' WAS THE LAST THING HE EVER DID

BENJAMIN DEWEY

TRAGEDY #485

INNOCENT INMATE TUNNELS OUT ON THE DAY OF CARNIVOROBOT UPRISING

TRAGEDY #486

PERCEPTIONS ASIDE, SHE'D RATHER NOT BE LONE

TRAGEDY #487

FLOWERY LANGUAGE WASN'T PERSUASIVE THIS TIME

TRAGEDY #488

ORIGINAL 5TH 'HORSEMAN OF INSULTS'
REACTS UNGRACEFULLY TO DISMISSAL

BENJAMIN DEWEY

TRAGEDY#489

ULTIMATE-SUSPENDERS PROTOTYPE
EXCEEDS EFFECTIVENESS EXPECTATIONS

TRAGEDY #490

SWEET-TOOTH SEALS MISUNDERSTAND
DOCTOR'S ADVICE ABOUT BALANCED MEALS

TRAGEDY #491

XII XIII XIV

THE YARNIAN ROYAL FAMILY COMES MORE UNSPOOLED AS GENERATIONS PASS

TRAGEDY #492

POSSESSED APPLIANCE TAUNTS BY WAFTING PHANTOM-WAFFLE SCENTS & PREVENTING THEIR PRODUCTION

TRAGEDY # 493

AXIOM AMENDED TO 'STRONG AS A KEVIN' FOLLOWING DEFEAT AT PUBLIC SHOWDOWN

TRAGEDY # 494

ENCHANTRIFICATION OF HISTORIC DISTRICT TROUBLES MANY LONGTIME RESIDENTS

BENJAMIN DEWEY

TRAGEDY #495

ISOLATION NARROWS STRANDED SIBLINGS' COURTSHIP OPPORTUNITIES

TRAGEDY #496

MIDDLE DISTANCE GOT A RESTRAINING ORDER, YET THE STARING CONTINUES

TRAGEDY #497

CAPTURED BIRD BETRAYS
BUSH-DWELLING COLLEAGUES

TRAGEDY # 498

CUDDLY RIVAL GIVEN LAST TWO
CINNAMON ROLLS FREE OF CHARGE

BENJAMIN DEWEY

TRAGEDY #499

SOLEMN SCULPTURES' FROWNS TURNED
UPSIDE DOWN BY SET OF SILLY SISTERS

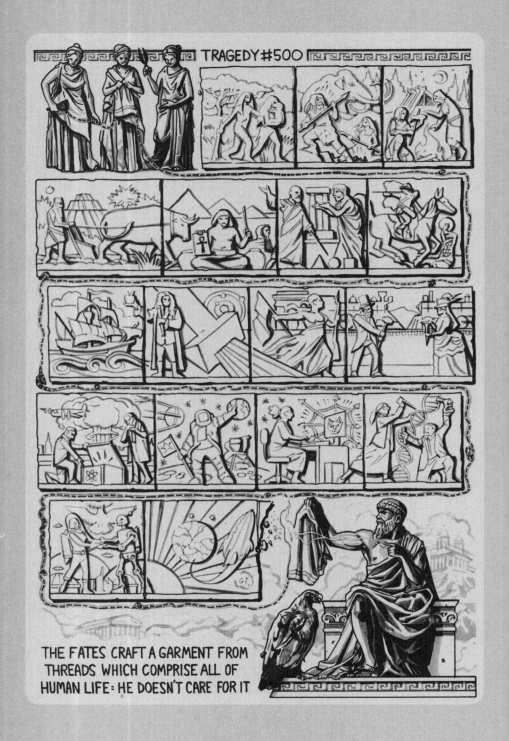

TRAGEDY #500

THE FATES CRAFT A GARMENT FROM THREADS WHICH COMPRISE ALL OF HUMAN LIFE: HE DOESN'T CARE FOR IT

BENJAMIN DEWEY

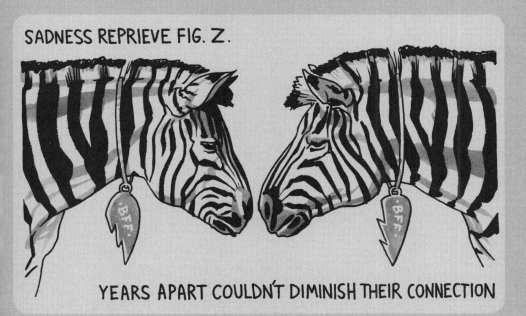

SADNESS REPRIEVE FIG. Z.

YEARS APART COULDN'T DIMINISH THEIR CONNECTION

TRAGEDY # 000*

HIS LIFE'S WORK MIGHT BE QUACKERY

* This Tragedy was initially rejected for being a simulacrum of the author's own experience and thus, a genuine tragedy.

SOME TIME AGO IN A PROPER PLACE CALLED HOURGLASS MANSION

THE QUEEN IS BESIDE HERSELF, LORD LIGHTNINGSPEAR!

THESE THREE OBJECTS ARE SIGNIFICANT TOKENS FROM HER SADDEST MEMORIES.

THEY'VE BEEN PILFERED!

A CURIOUS CASE INDEED, CONSTABLE PARKER.

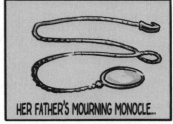

HER FATHER'S MOURNING MONOCLE...

FAVORITE FISH'S FORMER ABODE...

& MOTHER'S MIRROR OF SELF-CRITIQUE

HER MAJESTY WOULD LIKE THEM RECOVERED AND THE THIEF BROUGHT TO JUSTICE.

SHE ONLY TRUSTS ONE PERSON WITH SUCH A DELICATE CASE.

BENJAMIN DEWEY

BENJAMIN DEWEY

IT APPEARS TO BE AN INVITATION TO AN UNVEILING AND MASQUERADE FOR UNSAVORY CHARACTERS.

BACK TO THE SEWERS!

HOORAY!

THE EVIL EVENT OF THE YEAR:

WEAR YOUR BEST COSTUME OR MASK

WHERE: THE BRUMBLESHIRE MOORLANDS
WHEN: TONIGHT

WHY: TO ADV... THE CAUSE O...

CORDIALLY, G.S.

FROM THE LOOK OF THIS, WE'LL NEED ALL THE HELP WE CAN GET!

SOUNDS BLOODY AWFUL, EXCELSIOR!

WINGED FRIENDS, COME HITHER! I HAVE A TASK FOR YOU!

BENJAMIN DEWEY

BENJAMIN DEWEY

"I, **GENTLEMAN SKULL**, AM NOW THE MIGHTIEST."

"I'M THE KEEPER OF THE DETERMINATION-CAPE, BEARER OF THE WISDOM-HAT AND BEST OF ALL..."

"INVENTOR OF THE 'EYE OF JUDGMENT', WHICH CONVERTS SADNESS INTO **POWER**."

"I MELTED DOWN HER MAJESTY'S DEAREST ITEMS TO MAKE IT. THAT'S THE SECRET INGREDIENT!"

"I CAN SEE SOMEONE'S WORST MEMORIES, WHICH I THEN USE:"

"THE EYE CONVERTS STRENGTH THEY GAINED FROM ADVERSITY INTO ENERGY BLASTS OF LETHAL FORCE FOR ME!"

"MY OLD DOG."

"NO BIRTHDAY PRESENTS."

"SCHOOLYARD TAUNTS."

"LOST LOVE!"

"I'VE ALWAYS FED ON SADNESS, BUT WHERE I USED TO SETTLE FOR CRUMBS ON THE SURFACE, A FEAST CAN BE FOUND IN THE ONCE-HIDDEN DEPTHS."

"SO MUCH DESPAIR FOR A HERO!"

BENJAMIN DEWEY

BENJAMIN DEWEY was born in the latter years of the twentieth century in Cleveland, Ohio. The majority of his childhood was spent haunting the halls of the art museum, where his father worked, and in the company of many cats whenever possible. He learned to draw by studying classic illustrations, comic books and attempting to catch up to the intimidatingly advanced development of more talented rivals. He now lives in Oregon with fewer cats, far too many guitars, and a very supportive wife named Lindsey. This book represents an exhaustive map of his anachronistic, surrealist brain-scape.

These are the clues as they appeared in sequence in the online posts. If you wish to solve the puzzle on your own, don't look at the bottom of this page!

ODDS

TOMCIHONIIDNSENSRROTHGIEF
NSRTECOLFUYBEOGIBOATKLSNP
AOSEET

EVENS

RFORETTOTDAICEEPUYATNLEDA
EUARWLEROYDVLNEFTHEISEIPH
NIRH

To see solution hold this book upside down and look at reflection in a mirror

"THERE IS NO HAPPINESS LIKE THAT OF BEING
LOVED BY YOUR FELLOW-CREATURES, AND
FEELING THAT YOUR PRESENCE IS AN ADDITION
TO THEIR COMFORT"
— CHARLOTTE BRONTE
JANE EYRE